Woodstock Ontario Book 3 in Colour Photos, Saving Our History One Photo at a Time

Photography
by Barbara Raué
updated 2019

Series Name:
Cruising Ontario

Book 127: Woodstock Book 3

Cover photo: 84 Vansittart Avenue

Series Name: Cruising Ontario, Saving Our History One Photo at a Time in colour photos

Books Available in Alphabetical Order:
Aberfoyle, Acton, Ajax, Alton, Amherstburg, Ancaster, Arthur, Auburn, Aylmer, Ayr, Beaver Valley, Belfountain, Belgrave, Belleville, Bloomingdale, Blyth, Brantford, Brockville, Burford, Burgessville, Burlington, Caledon, Caledonia, Cambridge, Carlow, Cayuga, Chatsworth, Cheltenham, Clifford, Colborne, Collingwood, Conestogo, Delhi, Dorchester to Aylmer, Drayton, Drumbo, Dundas, Dunlop, Dunnville, Eden Mills, Elmira, Elora, Embro, Erin, Essex, Fergus, Fort Erie, Georgetown, Goderich, Grimsby, Guelph, Hagersville, Haldimand County, Hamilton, Hanover, Harriston, Hespeler, Ingersoll, Inglewood, Innerkip, Jarvis, Kingston, Kingsville, Kitchener, Lake Superior, Lincoln, Linwood, Listowel, London, Lucknow, Merrickville, Mono, Mount Brydges, Mount Forest, Mount Pleasant, Neustadt, New Hamburg, Newboro, Newport, Niagara-on-the-Lake, Niagara Falls, North Bay, Norwich, Oakville, Onondaga, Orangeville, Orillia, Oshawa, Otterville, Owen Sound, Palmerston, Paris, Parry Sound, Pelham, Perth, Peterborough, Petrolia, Pickering, Port Colborne, Port Elgin, Port Hope, Port Perry, Portland, Preston, Rockwood, Sarnia, Sault Ste. Marie, Seaforth, Sheffield, Shelburne, Simcoe, Smiths Falls, Smithville, Southampton, Southwest Oxford, St. Catharines, St. George, St. Jacobs, St. Marys, St. Thomas, Stoney Creek, Stouffville, Stratford, Strathroy, Sudbury, Tavistock, Terra Cotta, Thamesford, Thunder Bay, Tillsonburg, Toronto, Uxbridge, Waterdown, Waterford, Waterloo, Welland, Wellesley, West Flamborough, Westport, Whitby, Windsor, Wingham, Woodstock, York, Zorra

Book 125-127: Woodstock
Book 244: Woodstock Book 4
Book 238-239: Ingersoll
Book 240: Zorra Township
Book 241: Southwest Oxford
Book 242: Otterville, Burgessville
Book 243: Norwich

Woodstock is located in the heart of South Western Ontario, at the junction of highways 401 and 403, 50 km east of London and 60 km west of Kitchener. Woodstock is the largest municipality in Oxford County, a county known for its rich farmland, and for its dairy and cash crop farming. As well as being "The Dairy Capital of Canada", Woodstock also has a large industrial base, much of which is related to the auto manufacturing industry.

In 1792, Sir John Graves Simcoe became Lieutenant Governor of Upper Canada and made plans for the development of the interior of Upper Canada. To speed development in the sparsely populated interior of the province, Simcoe granted whole townships to land companies who were obligated to bring in settlers.

Settlement began in Woodstock in 1800. The early settlers were American immigrants from New York State. Increased immigration from Great Britain followed in the 1820s and 1830s, including the half pay officers Henry Vansittart and Andrew Drew.

By 1833 Nathaniel Hill had cleared thirteen acres in the area where Vansittart Avenue meets Dundas. He built the Royal Oak Hotel which burned down in 1852 and was replaced by a brick structure. Most of the big houses were built in the 1870s and 1880s with some replacing more modest structures and some built on undeveloped land. The trees that line Vansittart Avenue were probably planted in the 1880s. Vansittart Avenue was designed, and still remains, as a living monument to the Victorian ideal of gracious living.

Table of Contents

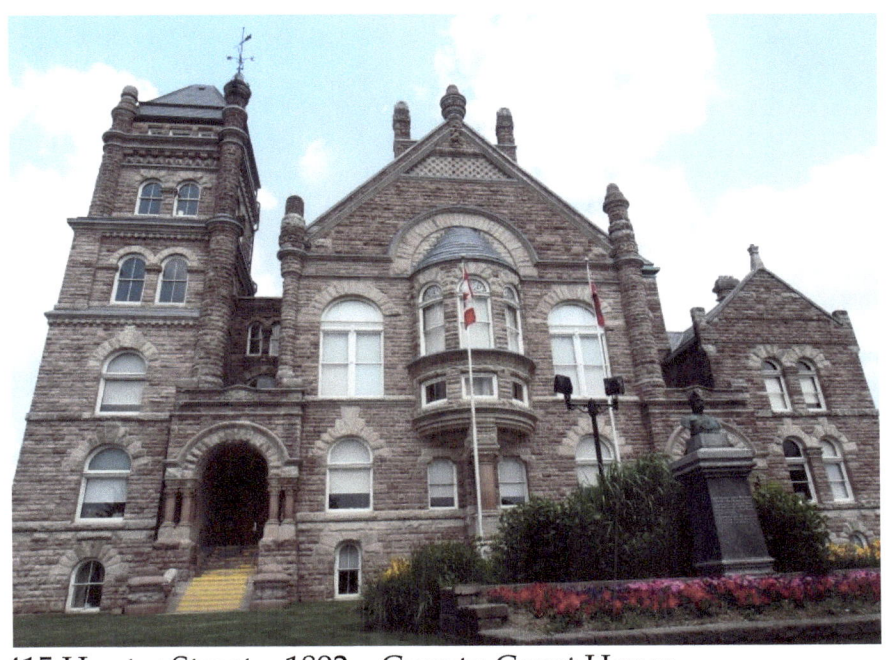

415 Hunter Street – 1892 – County Court House -
Richardsonian Romanesque style -2½ story, rose sandstone
with white sandstone lintels and drip molding, steep pitch
irregular slate roof, wall dormers with parapet walls topped
with finial, semi-circular windows above double hung
windows, recessed double doors, framed with Roman arch,
supported by pillars, two pillars have carved monkey heads,
2,2 story semi-circular bay windows, large stone newel posts
flank stairs, towers, turrets and elaborate chimneys, Centenary
stone mounted in the central buttress

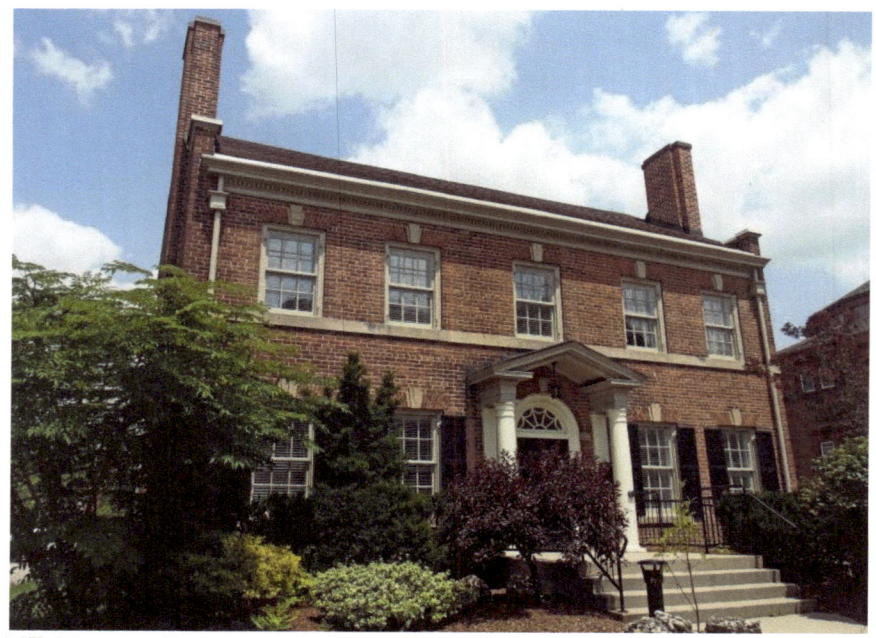

447 Hunter Street – 1913 - Neo-Georgian architecture, Neo-Classical door – symmetrical two story, red brick, once Presbyterian manse, parapet ends on gable roof, decorative stone keystone and stone

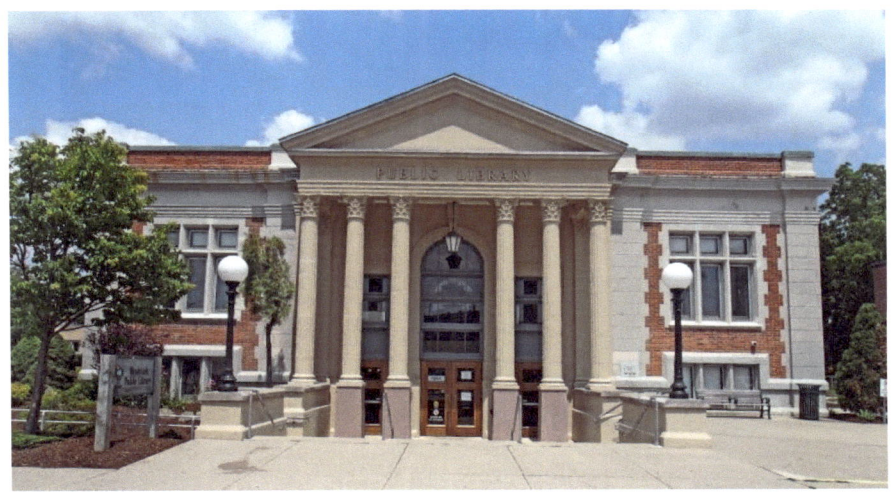

445 Hunter Street – Public Library – built in 1909 – Beaux-Arts Classicism style - brick, stucco on details such as quoins, columns, portico, Corinthian order columns with flutes, formed metal cornice, flat roof, Carnegie library

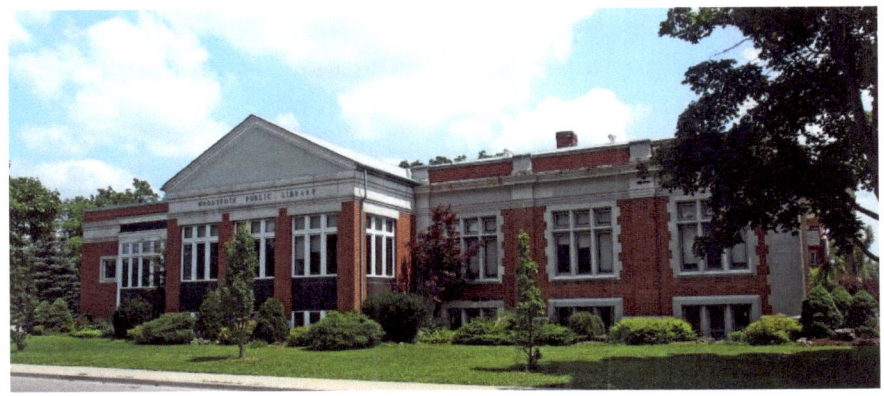

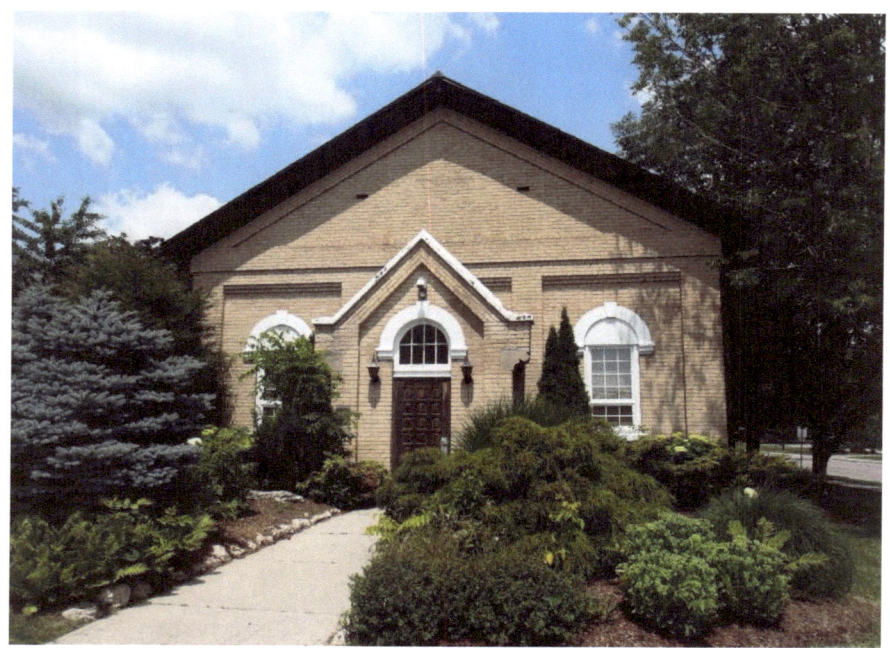

419 Hunter Street – 1876 – Vernacular - Old Registry Office, now housing Oxford County Social Services - slate gable roof, copper eaves, white brick, doorway and window are recessed with corbel bricking adding to symmetrical design, semi-circular lintels with keystone, closed porch repeats roof line and brick design, wall two feet thick and filled with sand for fire protection

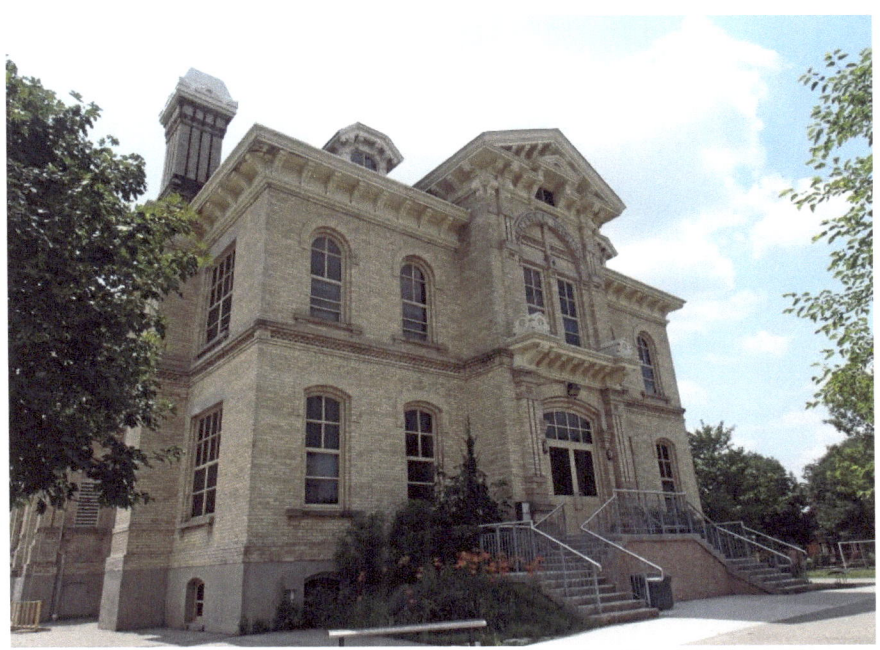

410 Hunter Street – Neo-Classical Revival - Central Public
School – built in 1880 – two story with useable attic, deep
wood eaves with decorated brackets, parapet with broken
cornice above main entrance, first floor window ellipse and
double hung, second floor semi-circular, double front door
with ellipse transom, name of school in stone above doorway
on second floor, decorated trunked chimneys with corbel
bricking, three entrances – boys, girls and teachers lead to
large spacious halls, all reached by steps

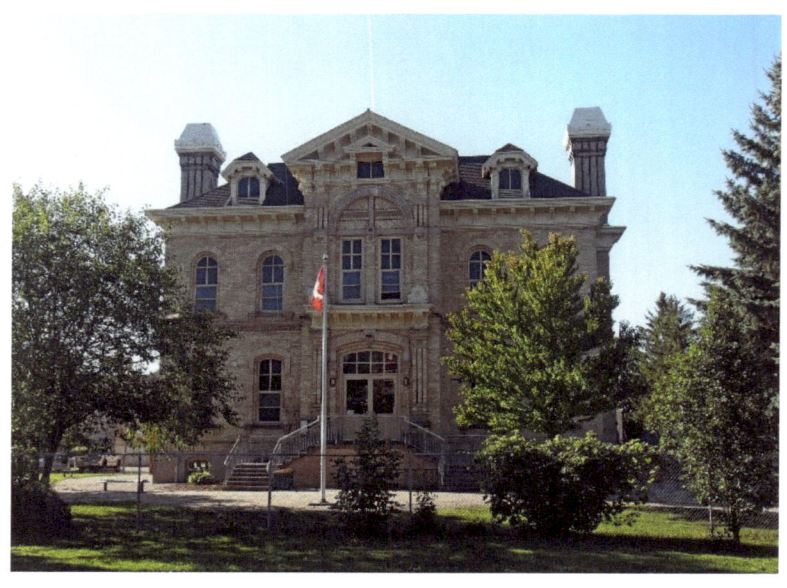

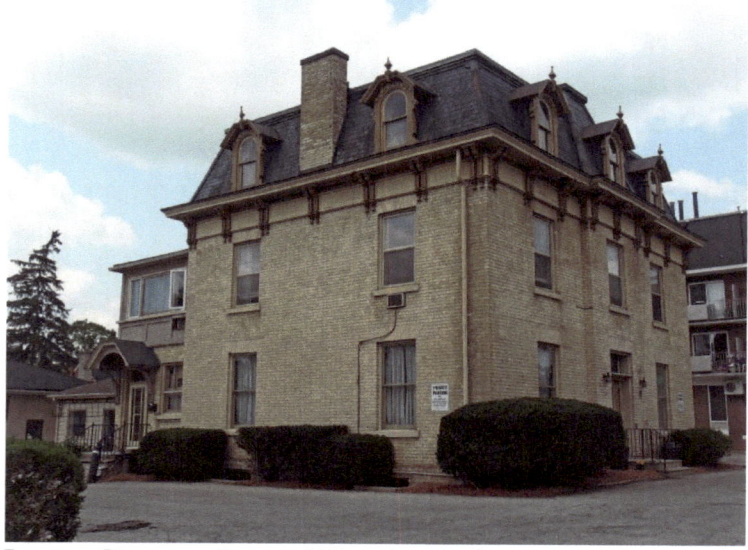

393 Hunter Street – Second Empire style – mansard roof with dormers with finials on window hoods, cornice brackets

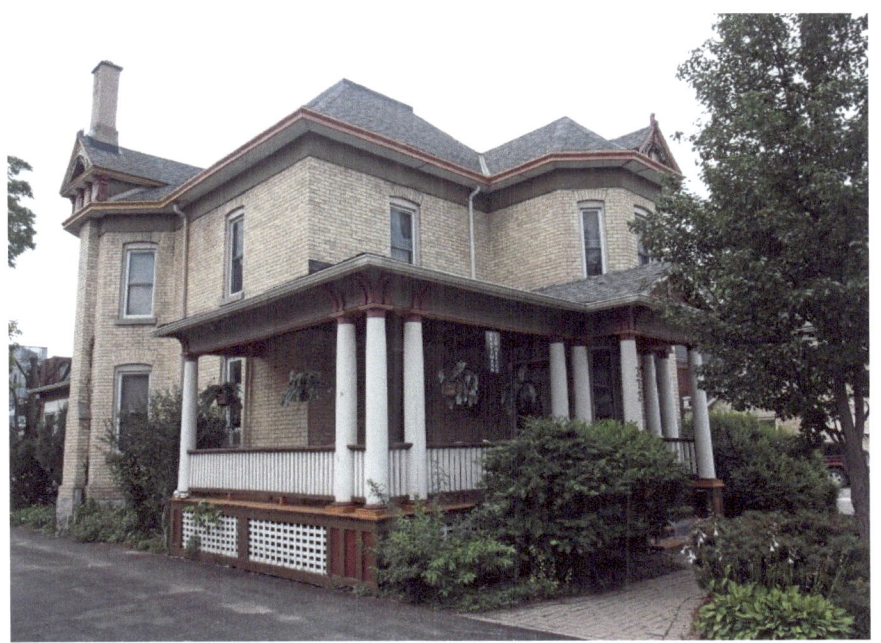

372 Hunter Street – Italianate – two story, white brick, trunked hip roof, decorated dormers with vergeboard with finials, two-story bay windows, off-center door with rectangular transom

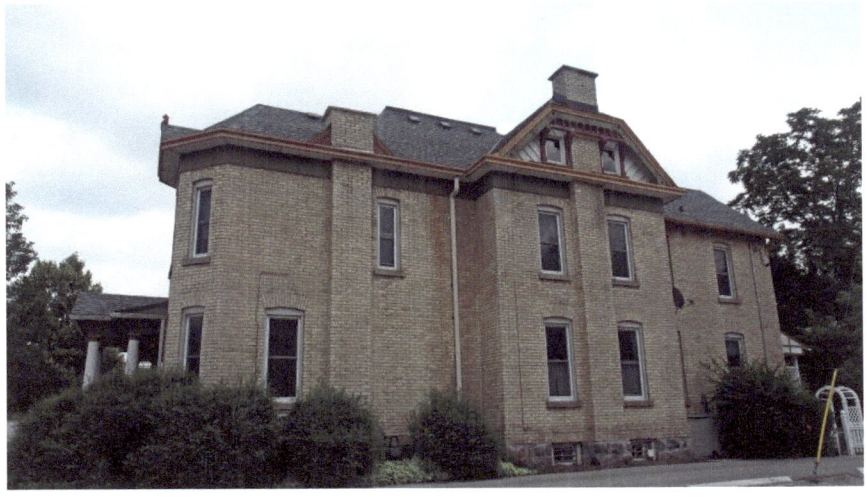

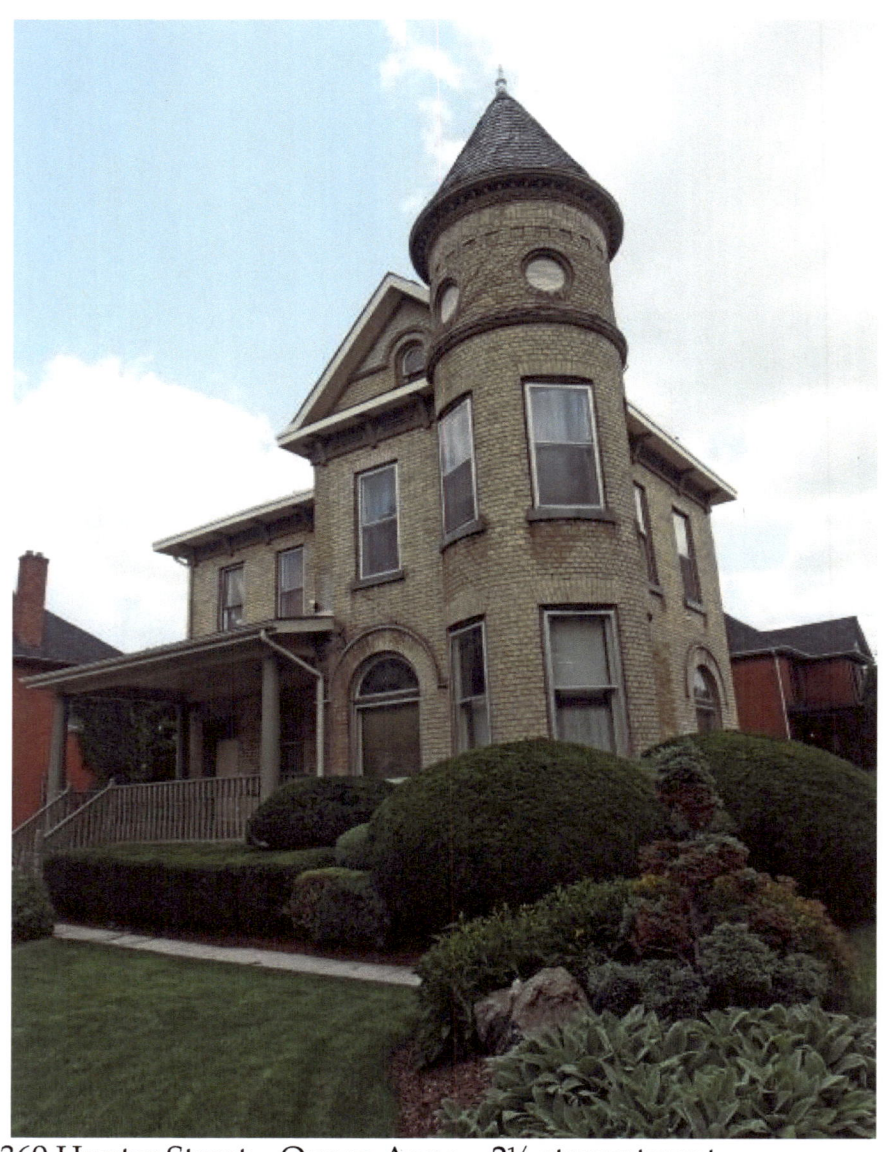

369 Hunter Street – Queen Anne – 2½ storey turret, Romanesque style window voussoirs, cornice brackets

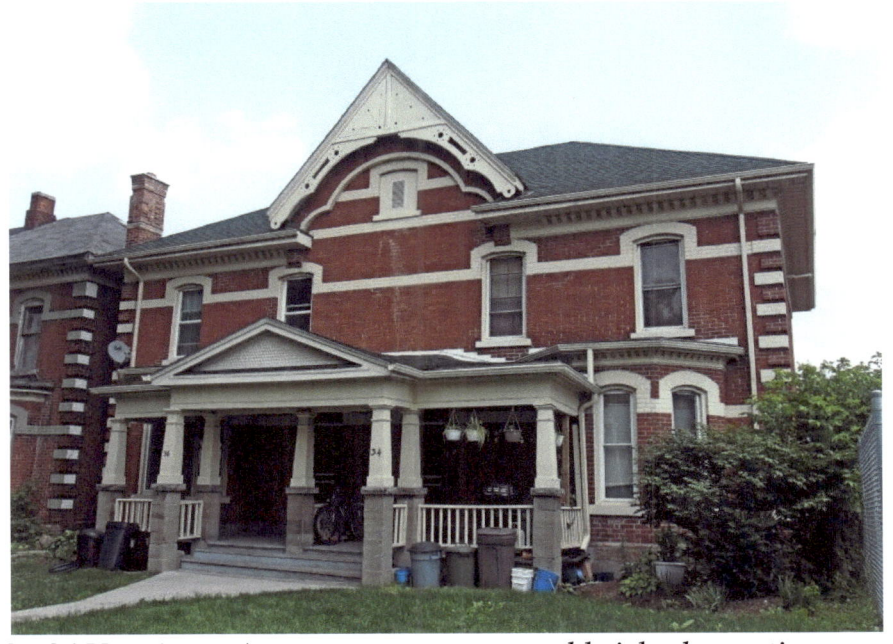

34-36 Vansittart Avenue – two story, red brick, decorative quoins, semi-detached, trunked hip roof, gable above entrance, deep molding repeats edging of vergeboard dentil on wide cornice, one-story bay window, centered paired doors, rectangular transom, tapered square posts support porch

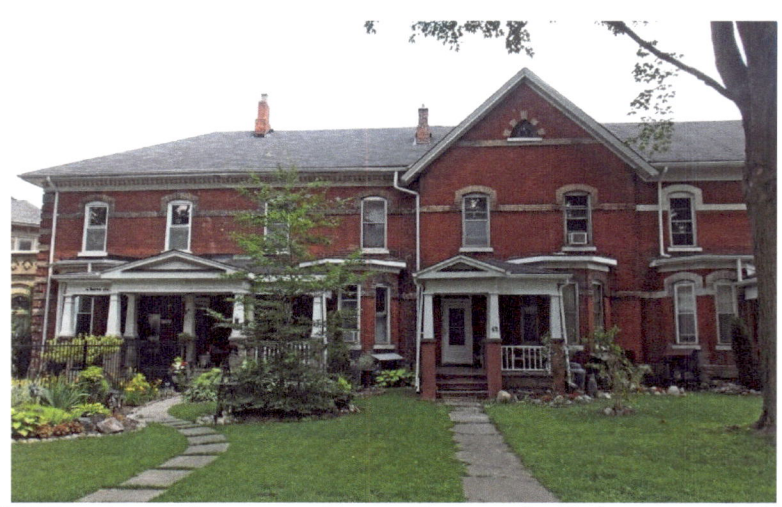

38-46 Vansittart Avenue – Peers Terrace built between 1888 and 1890 – two story red brick row housing, white brick trim, decorative quoins, hip roof, center unit has gabled entrance, ellipse heading transom, tapered columns support porch

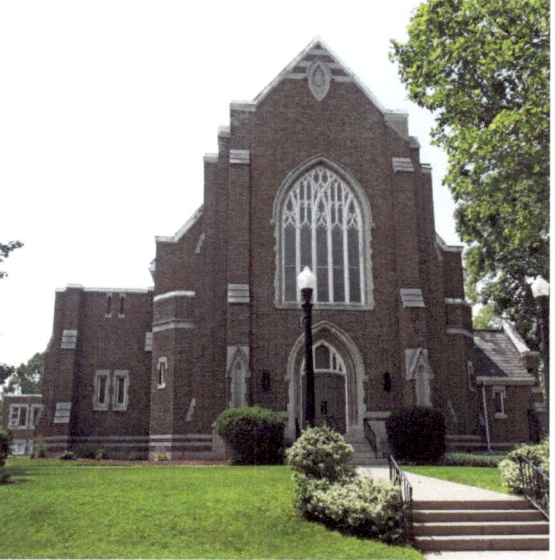

15 Vansittart Avenue – Chalmers United Church - now Koinonia Christian Fellowship – built in 1929 in the Gothic Revival style, buttresses

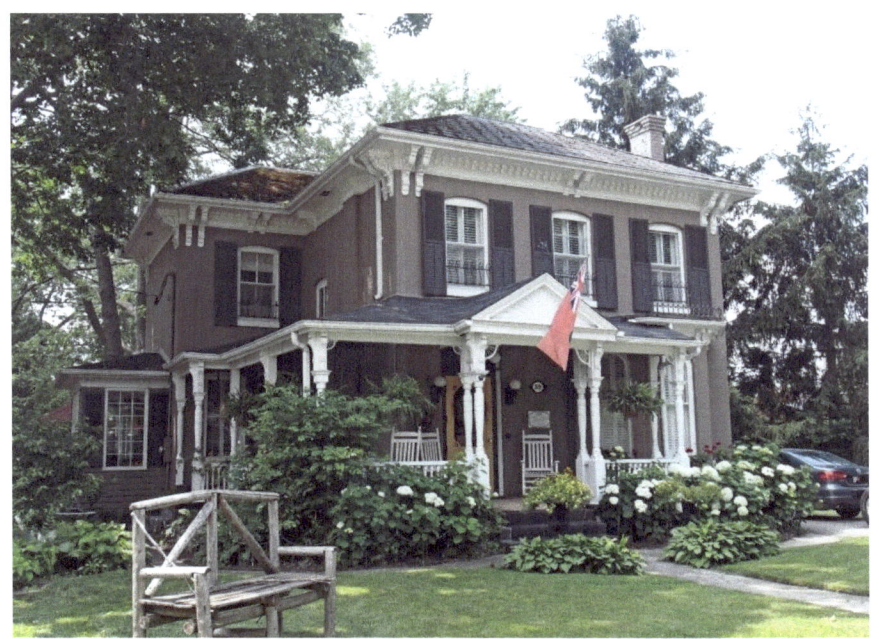

39 Vansittart Avenue – 1880 – Harry H. Powell, President
Woodstock Gas and Light Company - Italianate - two story,
painted brick, some bricks have paw prints, hip roof,
decorative dentils between paired brackets, one-story bay
window, decorative shutters, off-centered door, turned posts,
sunburst spindles, turned balusters, L shape verandah

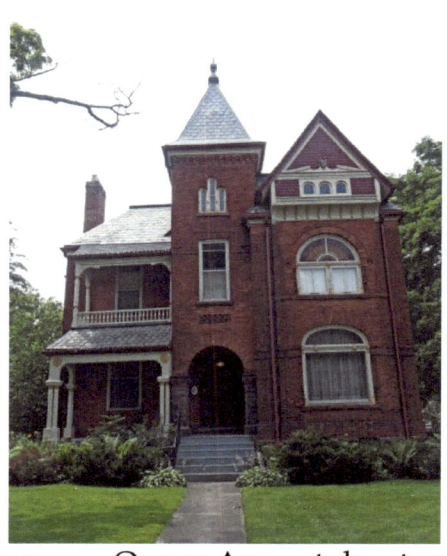

47 Vansittart Avenue – Queen Anne style – two story with attic, red brick, hip roof, painted red shingle decorative gables, door is protected by Roman arch of tower, paired posts support open side porch, turned posts and turned balusters, open balcony

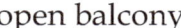

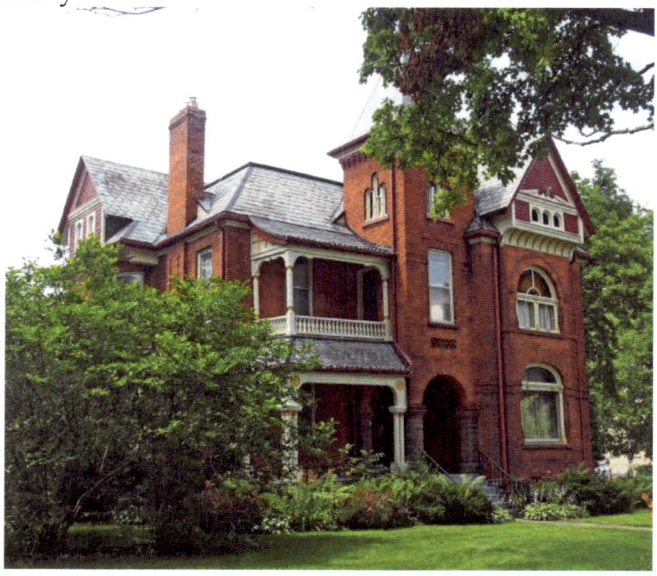

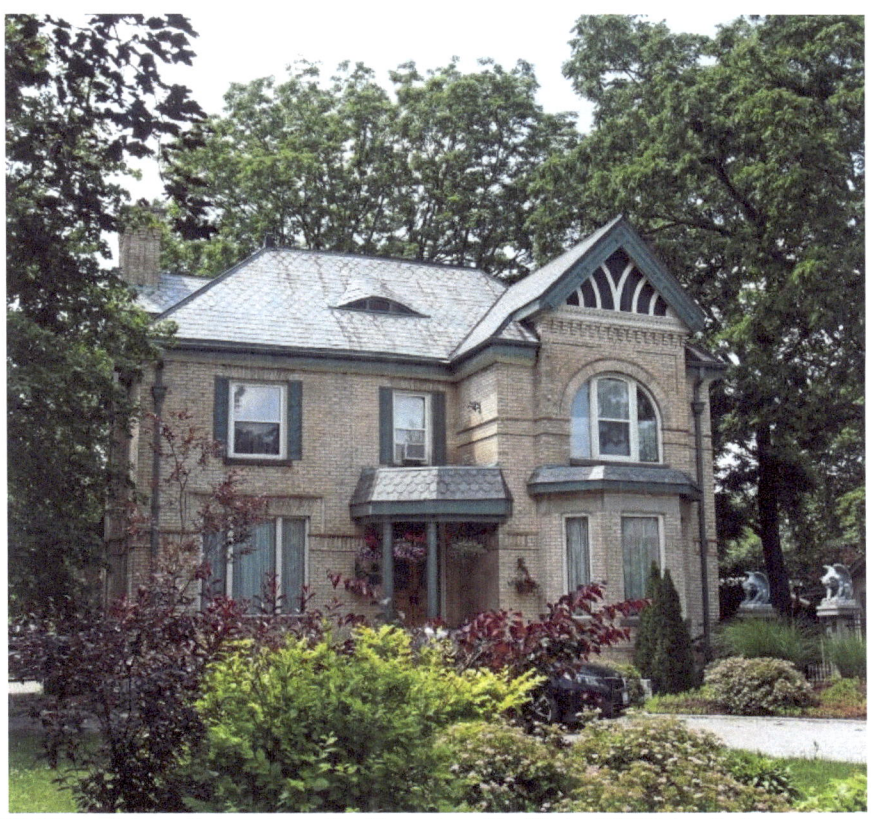

53 Vansittart Avenue – Italianate - Built in 1870 by John Forrest, proprietor of the Great Western Mills in Woodstock. The exterior of the building displays interesting brickwork in its walls and chimney with the unique "witches' eye" window on the east side. Two story with attic, white brick, trunked hip roof with gable door to exit, gable ends are timber boards and stucco, gable on south side has attic windows and beautiful corbel bricking chimneys, window is found between flues, drip molding with soldier brickery above windows, double front door with rectangular transom

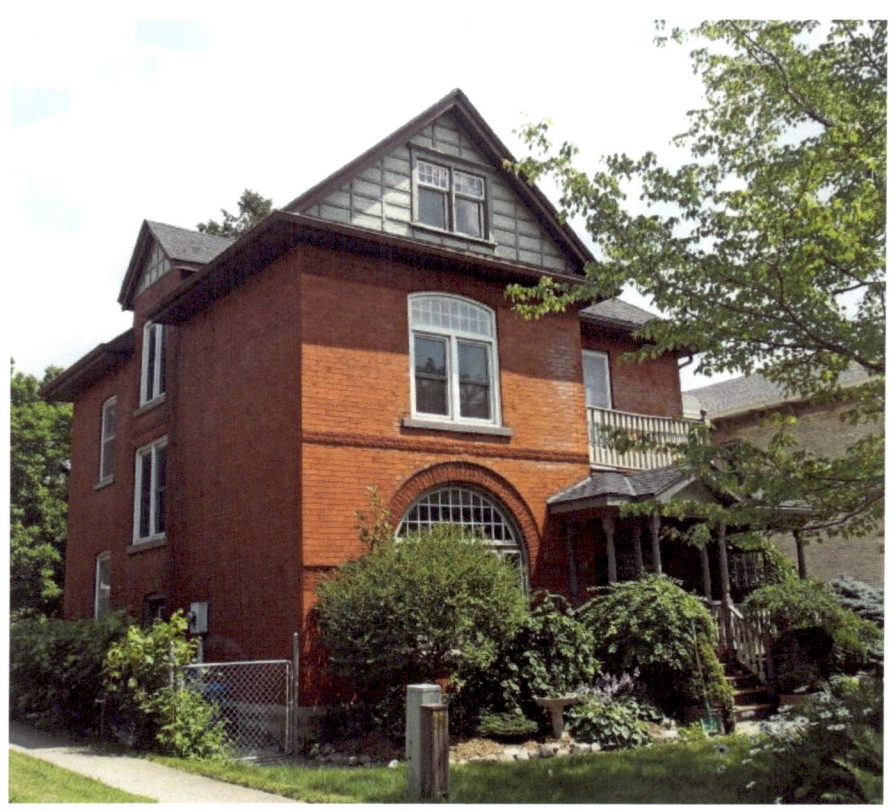

58 Vansittart Avenue – c. 1869 – Queen Anne – two story, red brick with dark red brick trim, painted wood trim in gable, hip roof, timbered gable, multiple lights decorate windows, Romanesque style window arch, semi-circular window tops three windows, segmental window tops two windows on second floor, 8-over-1 paired windows in gable, twelve lights in hall window, off-centered door, rectangular transom, with double doors in balcony, turned posts support open verandah and open balcony

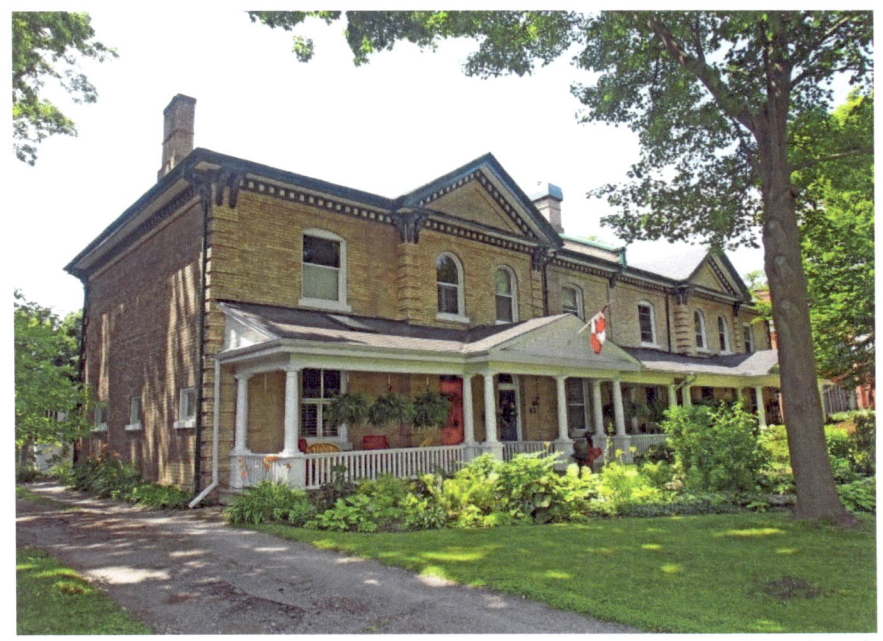

61-67 Vansittart Avenue – row houses - two story, white brick, decorative quoins, hip roof, gable above pediment in decorative dentils, semi-circular windows in projecting pediment, semi-circular transom, Doric pillars support verandah

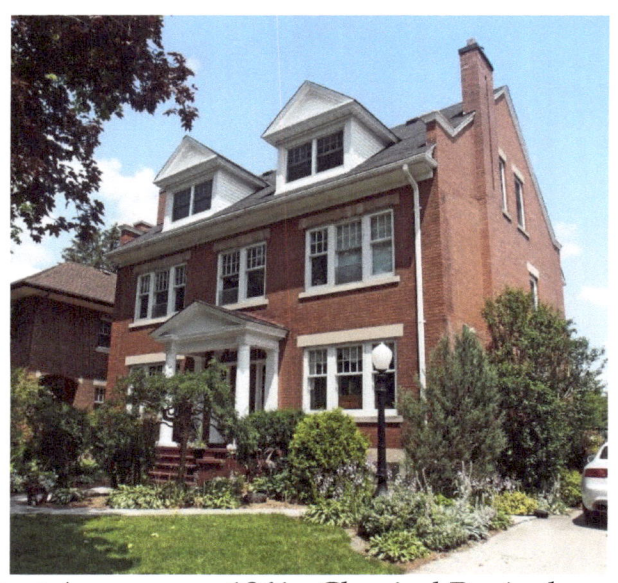

66 Vansittart Avenue – c. 1861 - Classical Revival - symmetrical two story with attic, red brick, gable roof, red shingle on paired dormers, stone sills and lintels, central door with side lights and transom, tall tapered Doric columns support open pediment style porch

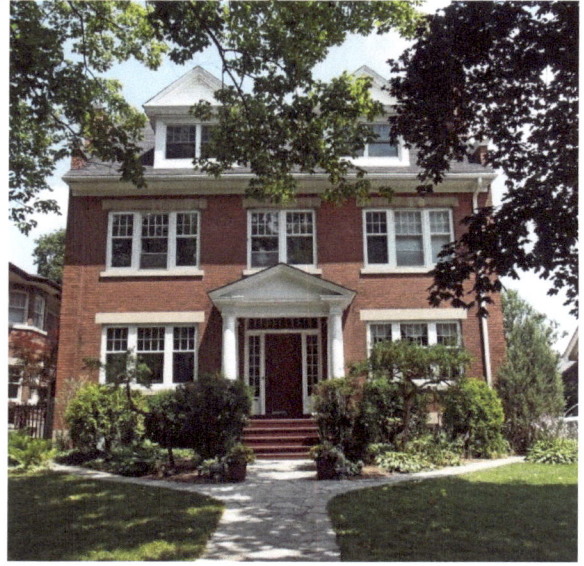

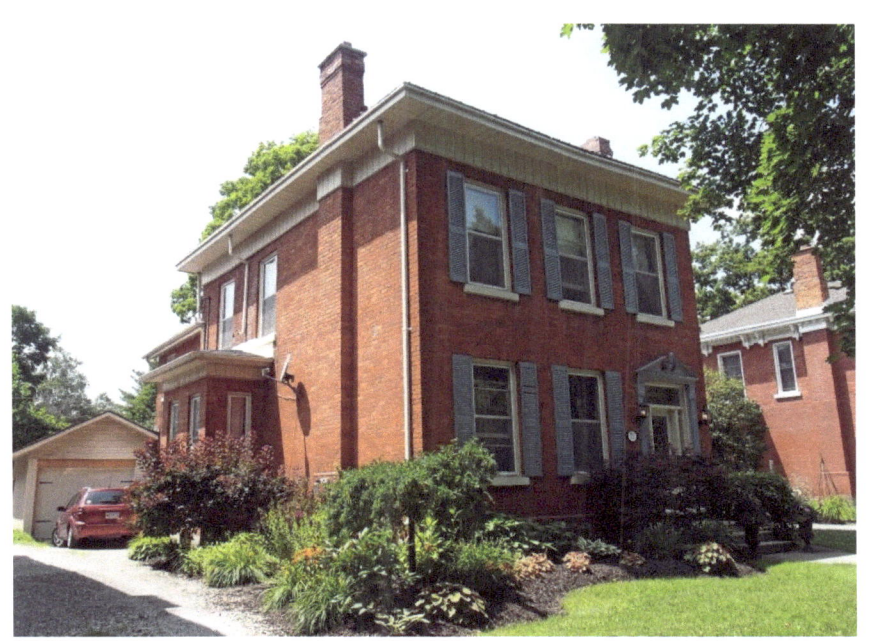

71 Vansittart Avenue – c. 1867 - Italianate - two story, cleaned red brick, hip roof, off-centered door with transom and sidelights

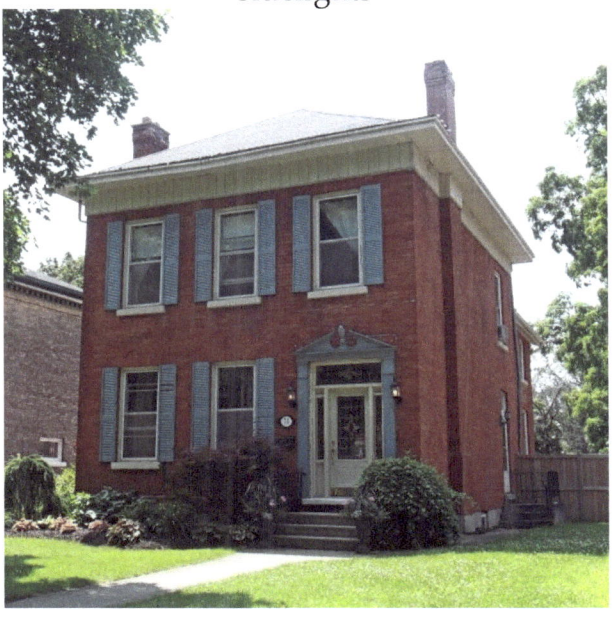

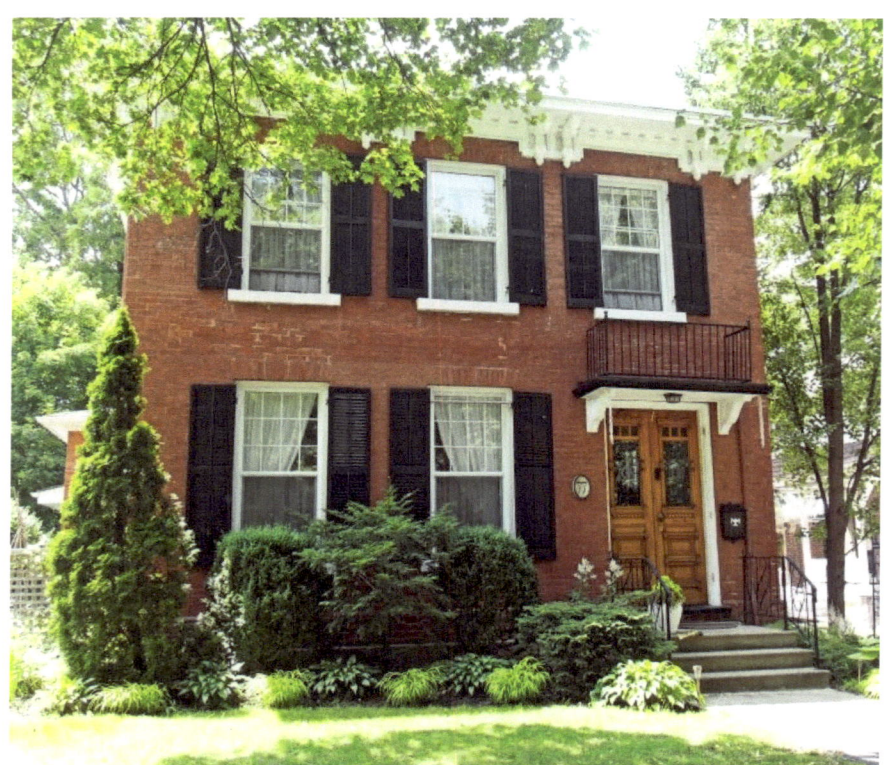

77 Vansittart Avenue – c. 1890 - Italianate - two story, red brick, hip roof, decorative dentils between paired brackets, off-centered double doors protected by flat hood

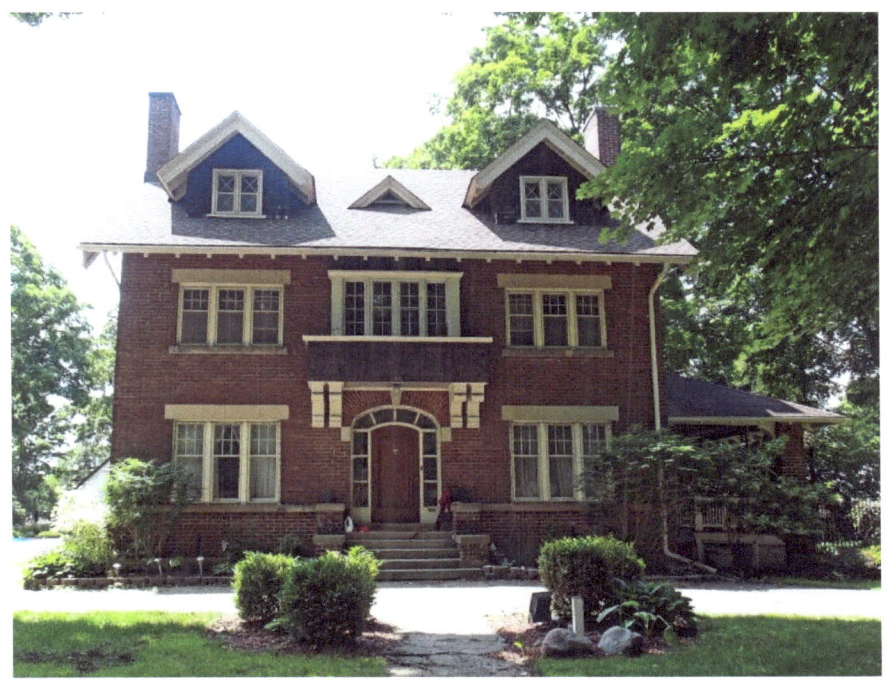

81 Vansittart Avenue – Colonial Revival - symmetrical two story with attic, dull red brick, gable roof has a pair of dormers separated by triangular window, stone sills and lintels, centered door with segmental top flanked with side lights and ellipse transom, oriel 4-over-4 windows supported with paired thick brackets

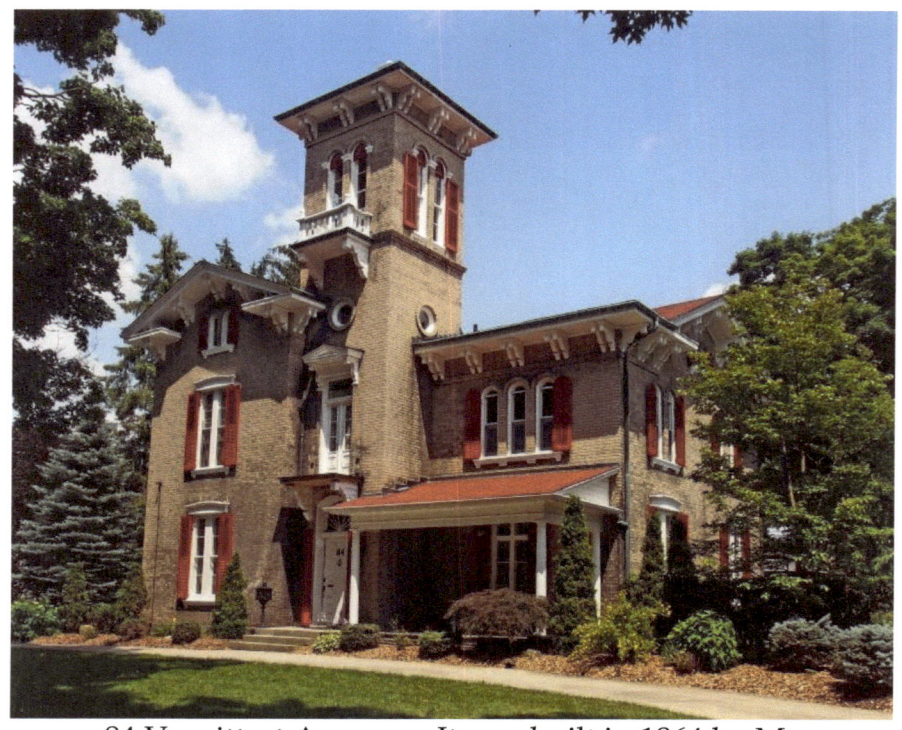

84 Vansittart Avenue – It was built in 1864 by Mr. Thomas H. Parker, a prominent merchant and first president of the Board of Trade in 1877. Mr. Parker was Mayor of Woodstock in 1878 and 1879. In 1911, Mr. M. W. Rowell was leader of the Ontario Liberal Party and resided here during his term as provincial member for Oxford.

Italianate villa - two story with attic, white brick, low pitch gable roof, deep eaves supported by paired brackets, windows grouped, first floor 2-over-2 flat, second floor 1-over-1 flat, decorative wooden lintels, sills supported with brackets, semi-circular windows on second floor, door in tower, segmental transom, hood supports balcony, Doric columns support side verandah, squared off-centered tower has hip roof ending in decorative finial

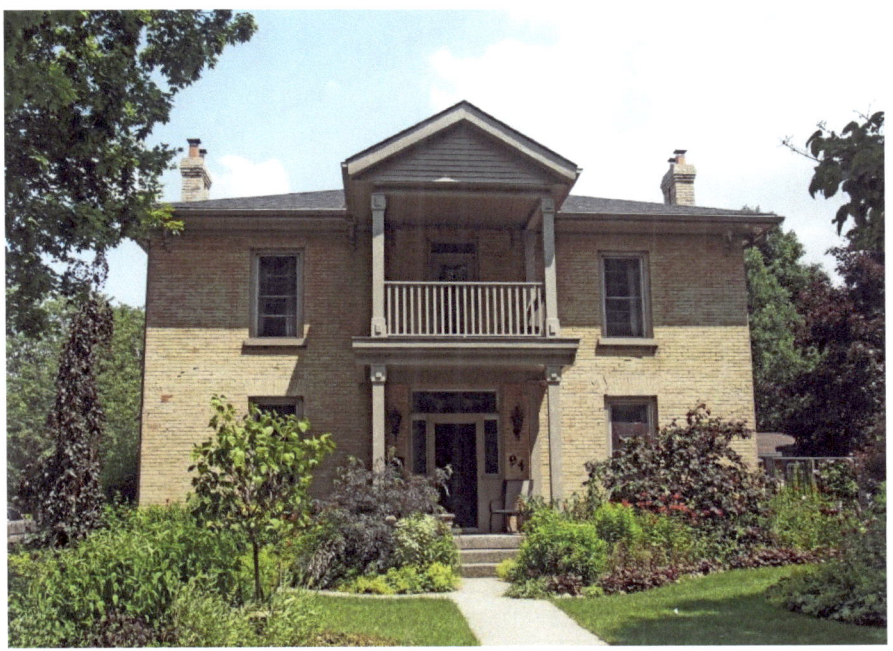

94 Vansittart Avenue – c. 1861 - Neo-classical - symmetrical two story, white brick, trunked hip roof, sparsely placed brackets, flat windows, centered door with stained glass side lights and transom

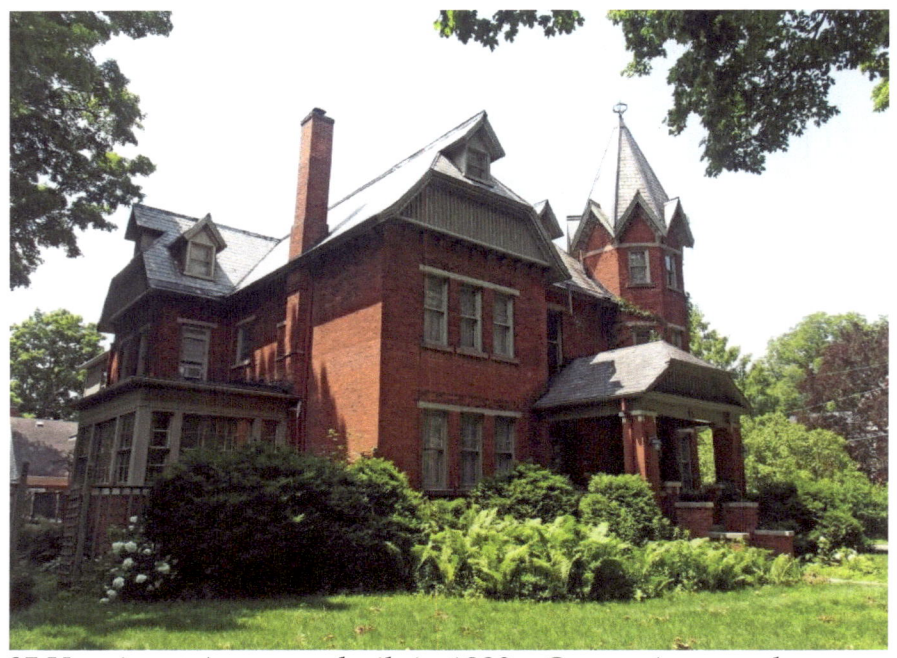

95 Vansittart Avenue – built in 1880 – Queen Anne style - two story with attic, red brick, trunked hip roof, evenly placed brackets surround the eaves, grouped stone lintels, six-sided three-story tower topped with gabled six-sided tower, center door with rectangular three-light transom, sturdy brick pillars support open porch

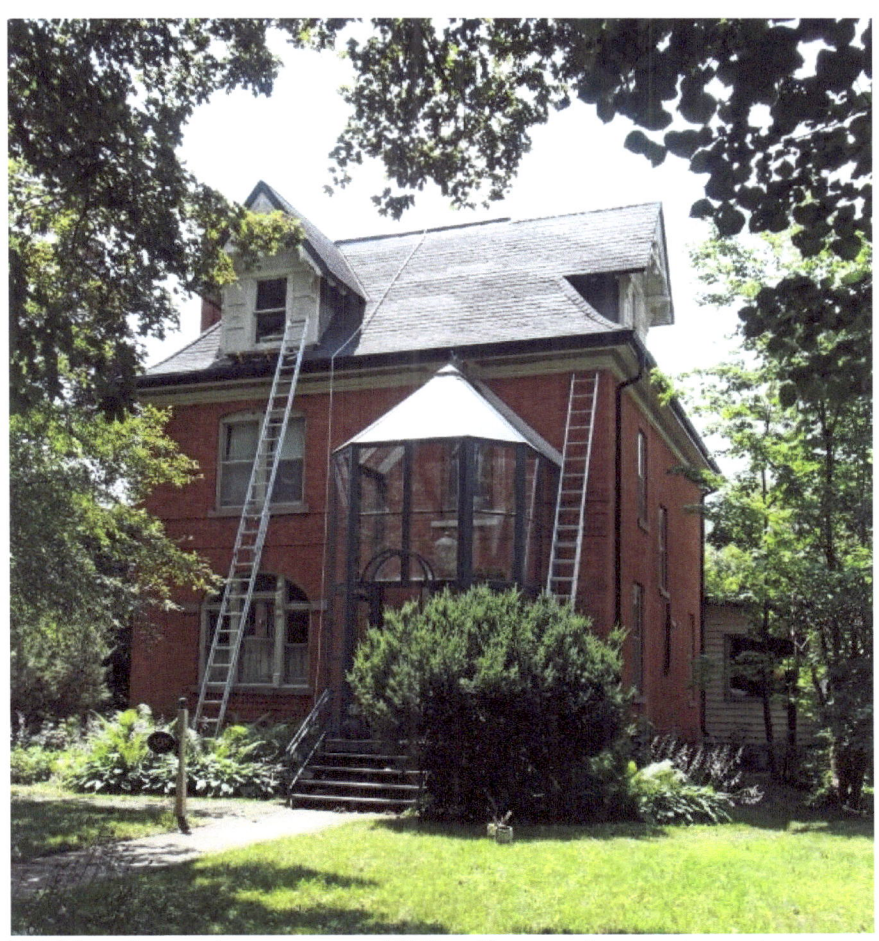

105 Vansittart Avenue – c. 1885 – Queen Anne - two story with attic, cleaned red brick, decorative brick string course on chimney and below windows, gable roof, gabled dormers, pendant post between vergeboard, windows grouped, semi-circular window has turned posts between windows, decorative corbel chimney and below windows, new conservatory 1992

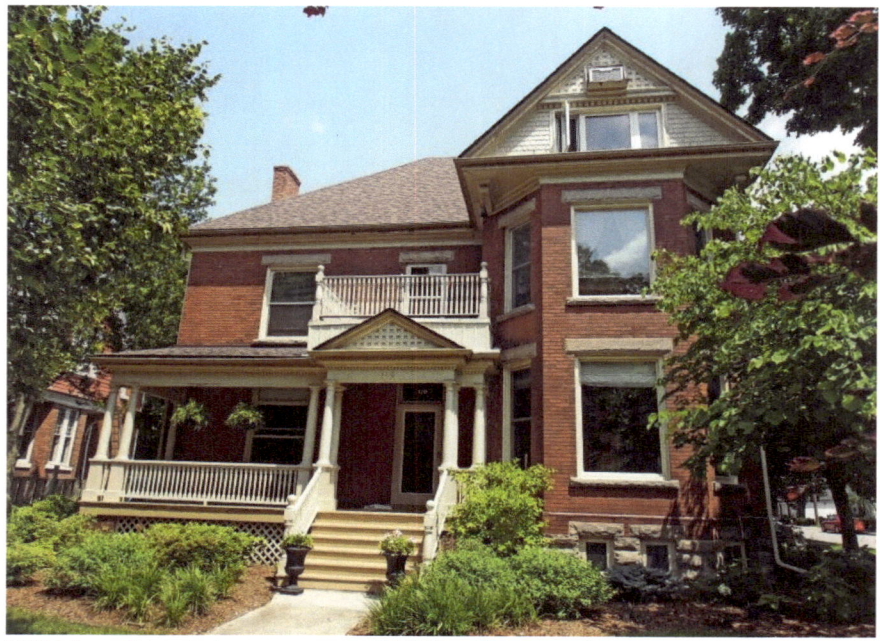

110 Vansittart Avenue – c. 1877 – Queen Anne - two story, red brick, painted white shingles on gable over bay window, trunked hip roof, painted white shingles in gable end, flat windows in two-story bay, stone lintels and sills, center door, stained glass transom, tapered Doric paired columns and turned balusters support verandah and balcony

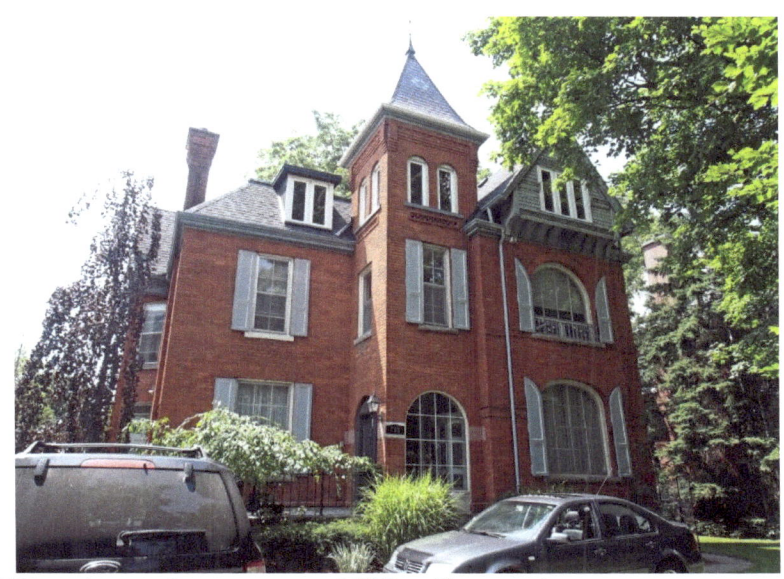

113 Vansittart Avenue – c. 1885 – Queen Anne - two story with useable attic, cleaned red brick, trunked hip roof, decorative shutters

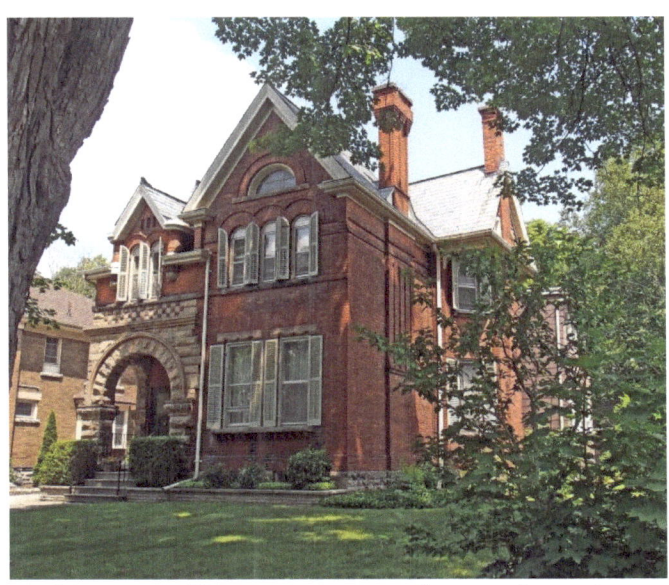

Vansittart Avenue – Romanesque arch, cornice return on large gable with semi-circular window, shutters

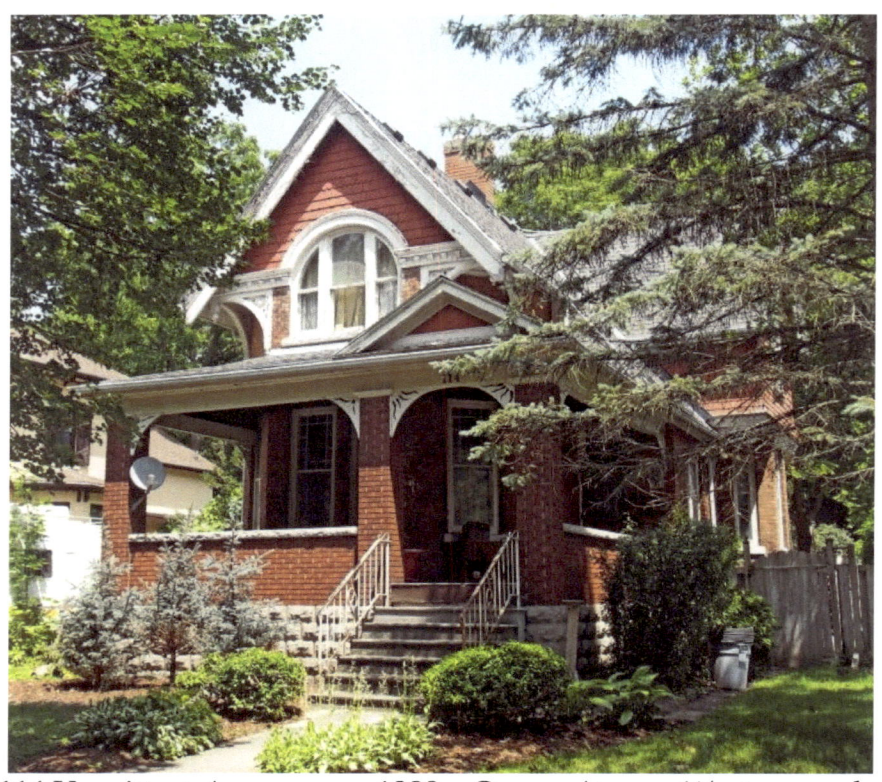

114 Vansittart Avenue – c. 1888 – Queen Anne - 1½ story, red brick, painted blue shingles on gables, gable roof, decorated cantilever brackets on gables, one-story bay window, second floor semi-circular window, off-centered door, sturdy brick pillars support L shape verandah, cantilever brackets

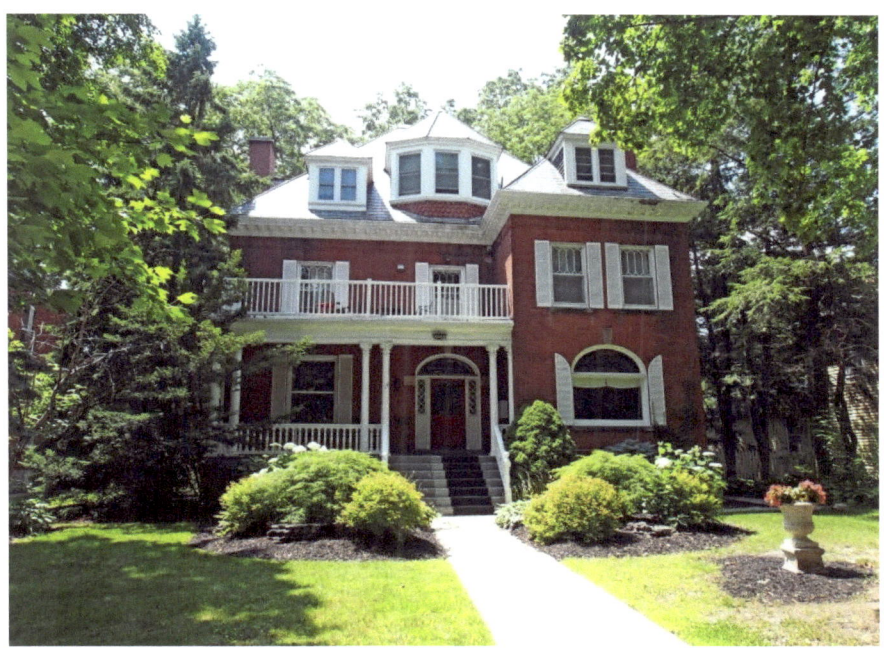

119 Vansittart Avenue – c. 1894 – Queen Anne – two story with useable attic, red brick, hip roof, large scotch dormer with hip roof dormers, dentils surround edge of roof, decorative shutters, stained glass in semi-circular front window, multiple lights in flat windows, centered door with beveled glass side lights and semi-circular stained glass transom, paired collared Doric pillars support open verandah and open balcony, turned balusters on verandah

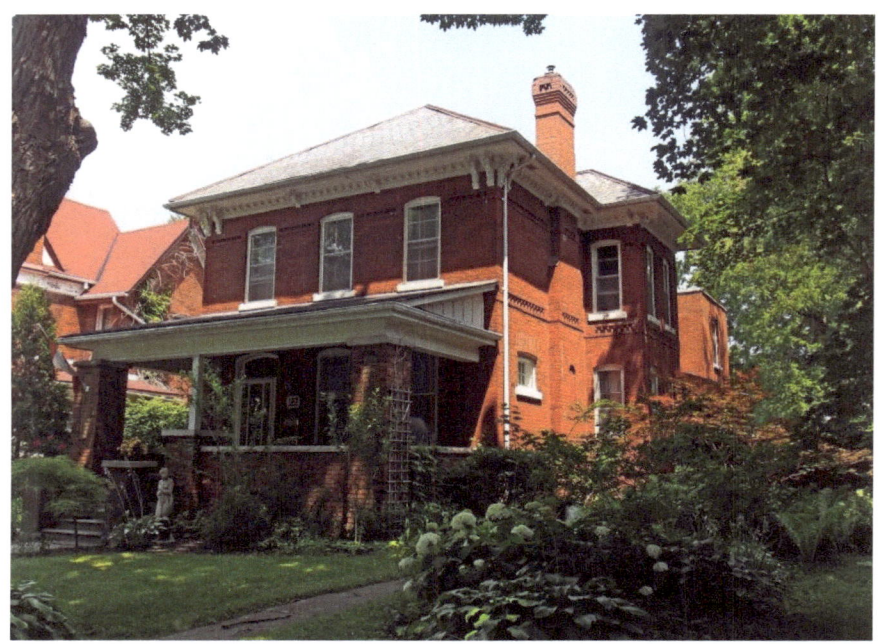

122 Vansittart Avenue – c. 1885 - Italianate, Edwardian - two story, red brick, decorative brick string course, hip roof, dentils with paired brackets on corners, off-centered door, stained glass transom, sturdy brick pillars support verandah, decorative string course, corbel bricking on chimney

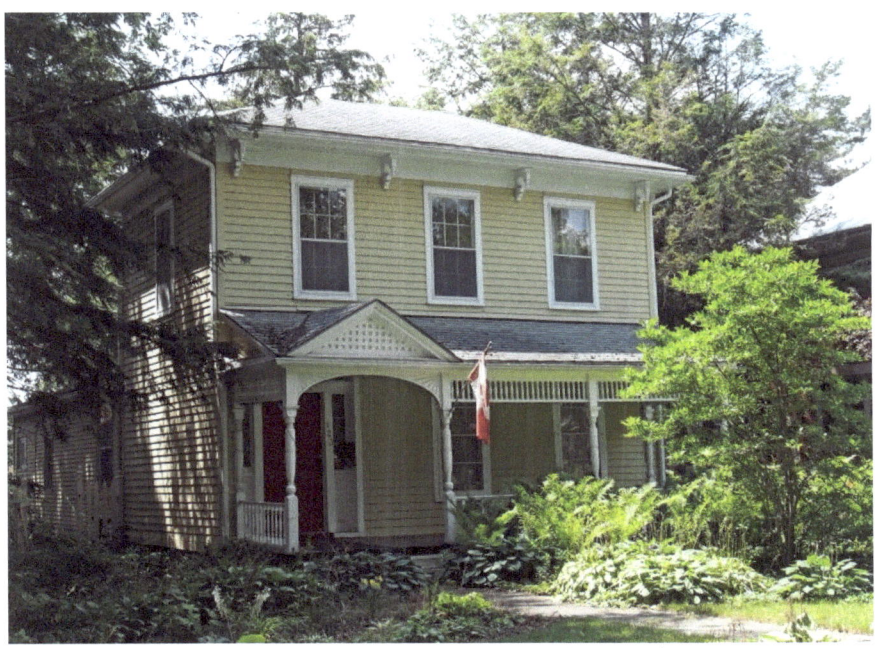

123 Vansittart Avenue – c. 1860s - Neo-classical - two story, trunked hip roof, single brackets, 9-over-9 flat windows, off-centered door flanked by side lights and rectangular transom, turned posts and spindles and balusters support verandah

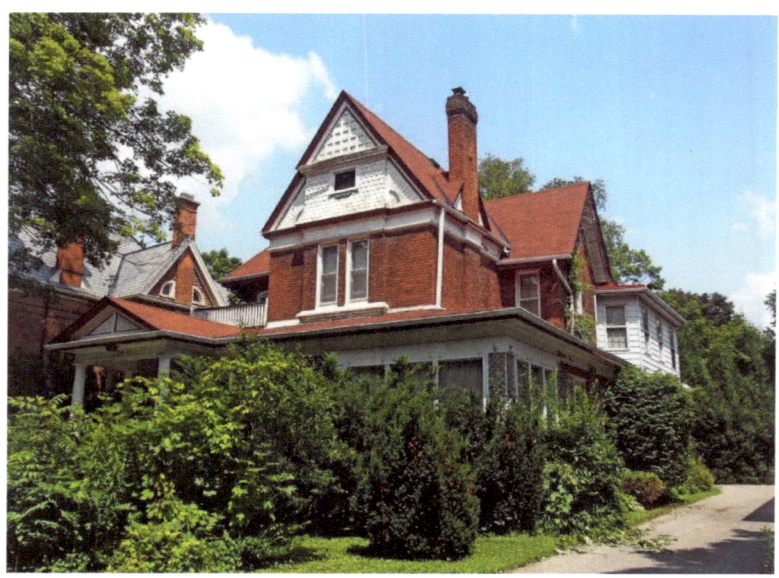

126 Vansittart Avenue – c. 1886 – Queen Anne - two story, red brick, painted white fish scale shingles, decorative wood sunburst in gable, decorated wood along trunked edge of hip roof, off-centered door, tapered Doric pillars support open/closed verandah and open balcony

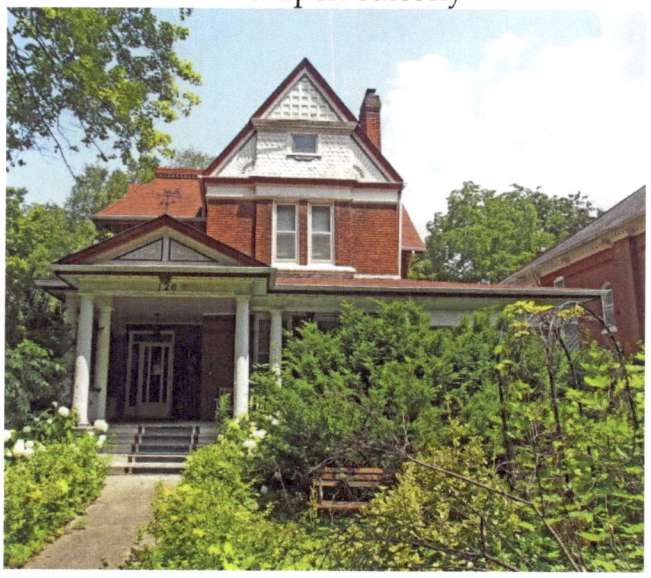

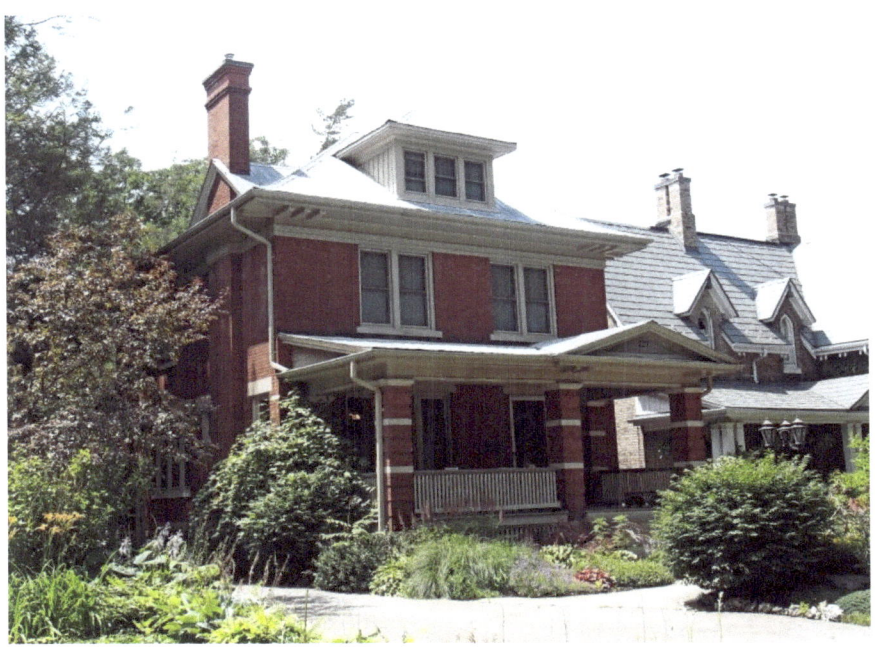

127 Vansittart Avenue – c. 1860s - Edwardian - two story with attic, red brick, hip roof, dormers, 12-over-1 flat windows are grouped, off-centered door, strong brick and stone pillars support open verandah with turned balusters and lattice skirt

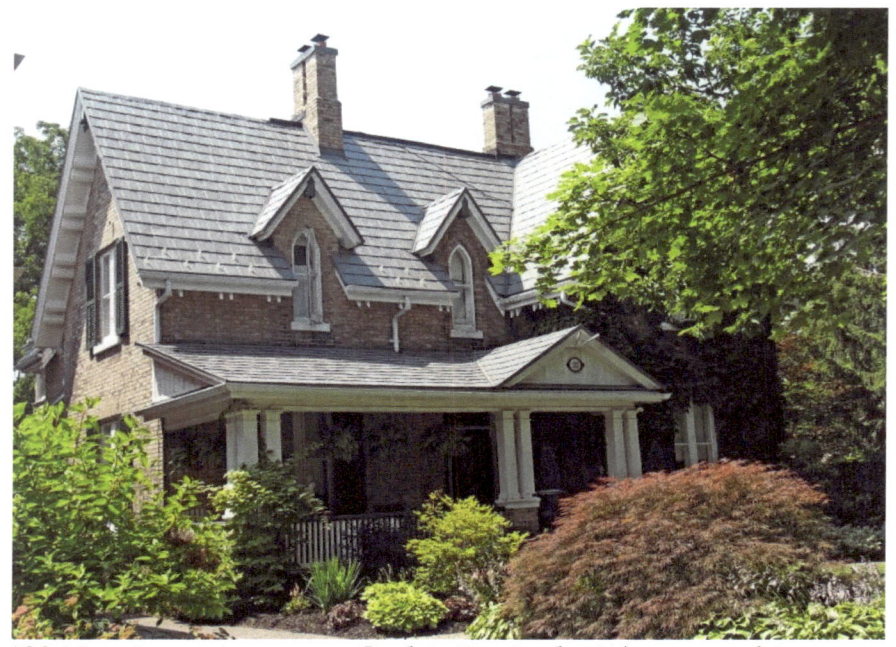

133 Vansittart Avenue – Gothic Revival - 1½ story, white brick, steep pitched gable roof with decorative paired exposed rafters, Gothic wall dormers and roof ends decorated with finials, flat windows grouped, centered door, rectangular transom, decorative shutters, paired square pillars support open verandah

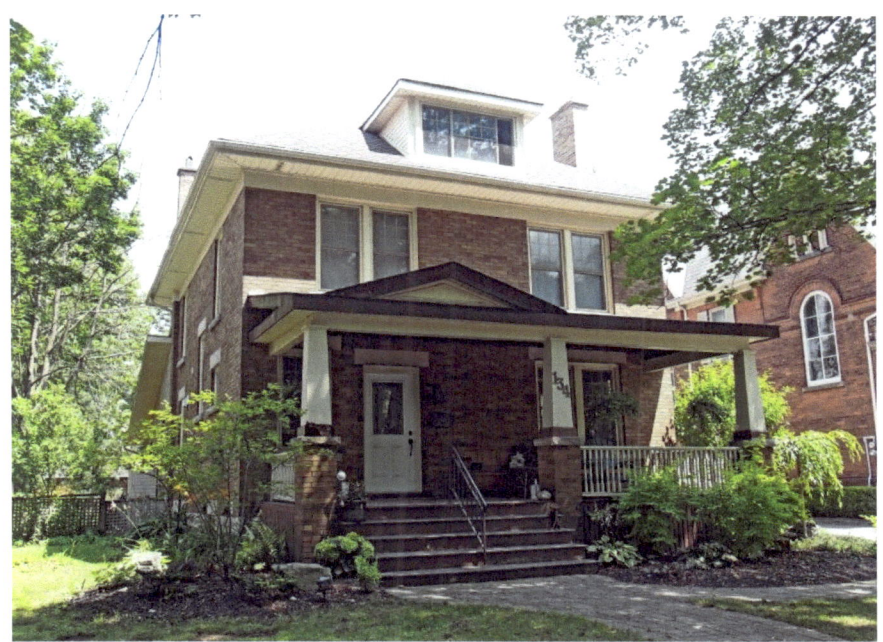

134 Vansittart Avenue – c. 1860s – Edwardian - two story with useable attic, buff brick, hip roof, front dormer, 12-over-1 flat windows grouped, stone sills, off-center door, tapered square pillars support open verandah

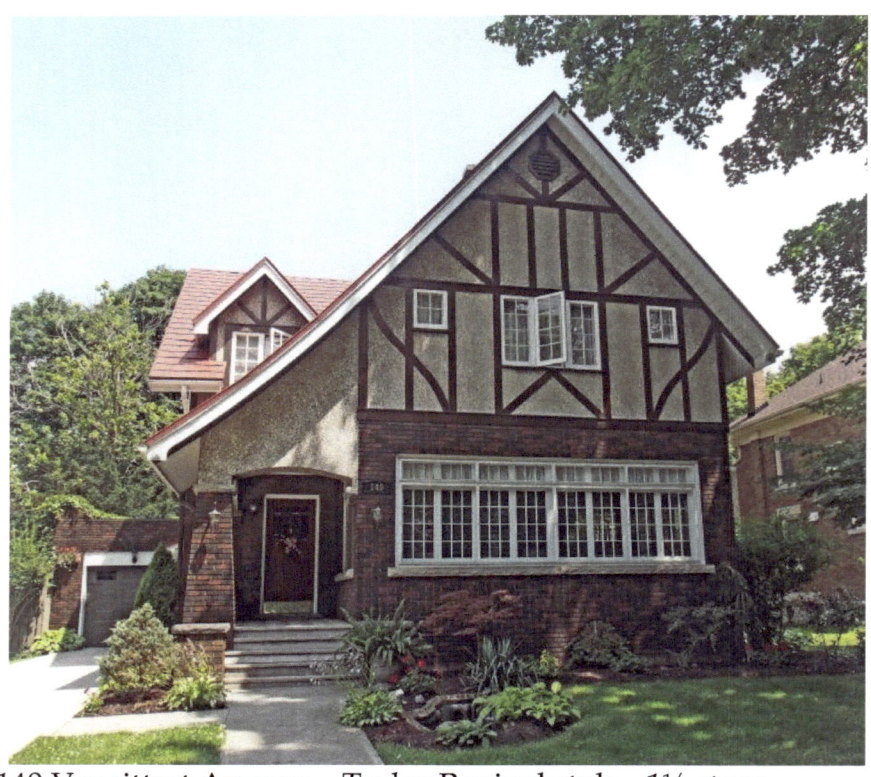

140 Vansittart Avenue – Tudor Revival style - 1½ story, stucco/timber in gables, salt box roof and gable roof at rear with gable wall dormer, multi-lights in grouped casement windows, off-centered door

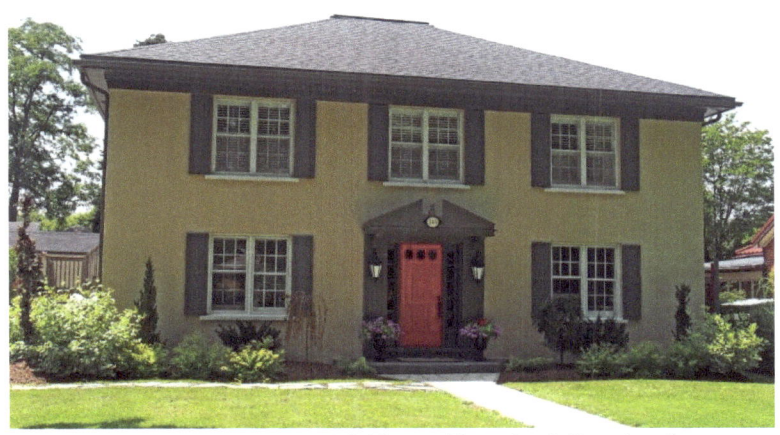

145 Vansittart Avenue – c. 1860s – Classical Revival - symmetrical two story, grey painted stucco, hip roof, flat windows grouped in pairs, decorative shutters, center door with side lights

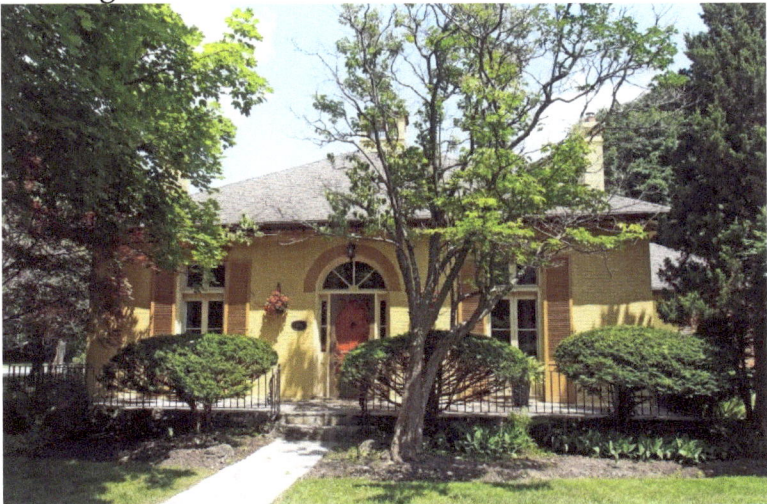

146 Vansittart Avenue – Regency cottage built in 1853 – one story with useable attic, painted brick, hip roof, lantern window lights, double French door with rectangular transom, center door has side lights and fan transom, semi-circular arch

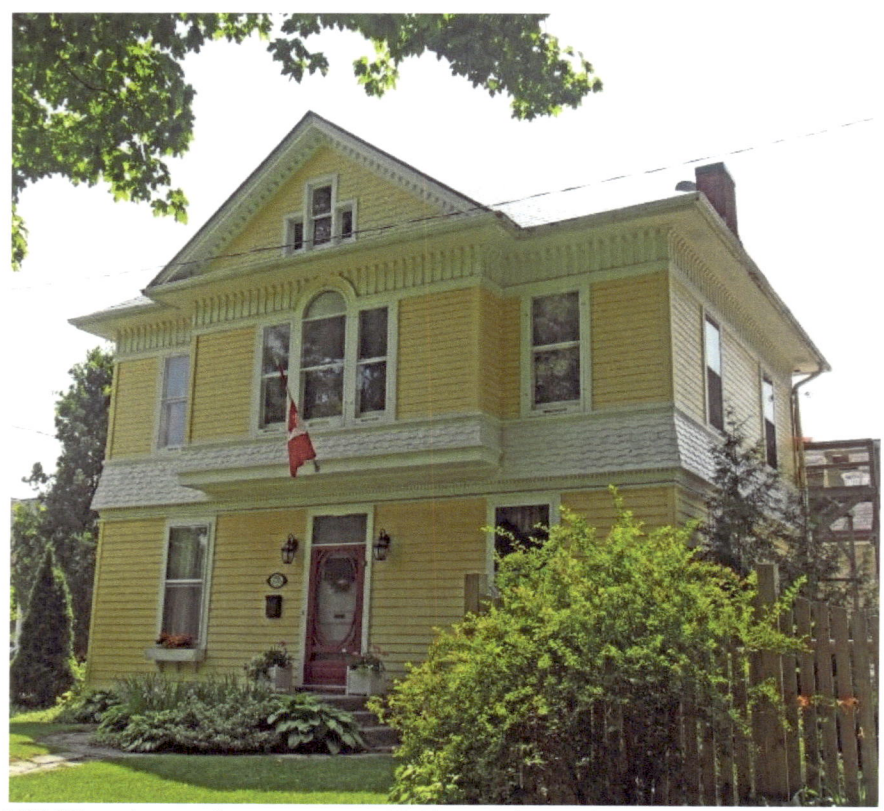

155 Vansittart Avenue – c. 1860s - Edwardian - symmetrical two story with attic, painted wood siding with decorative shingles between floors, steep hip roof, gable dormer, deep cornice and dentils, 1-over-1 rectangular windows with Palladian center window, centered door with rectangular transom, cement platform porch

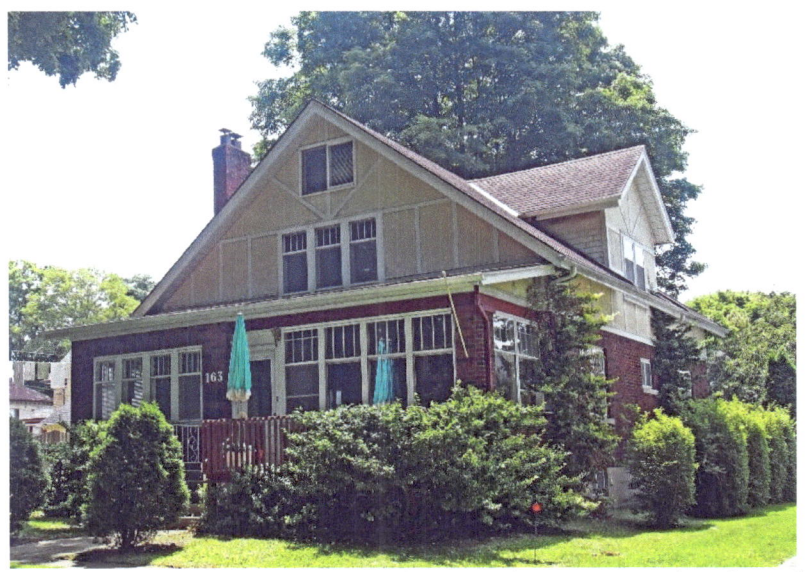

163 Vansittart Avenue – Bungalow - 1½ story, rug brick, gable roof with shed roof on closed verandah, stucco and timber in gable end, gable side dormer

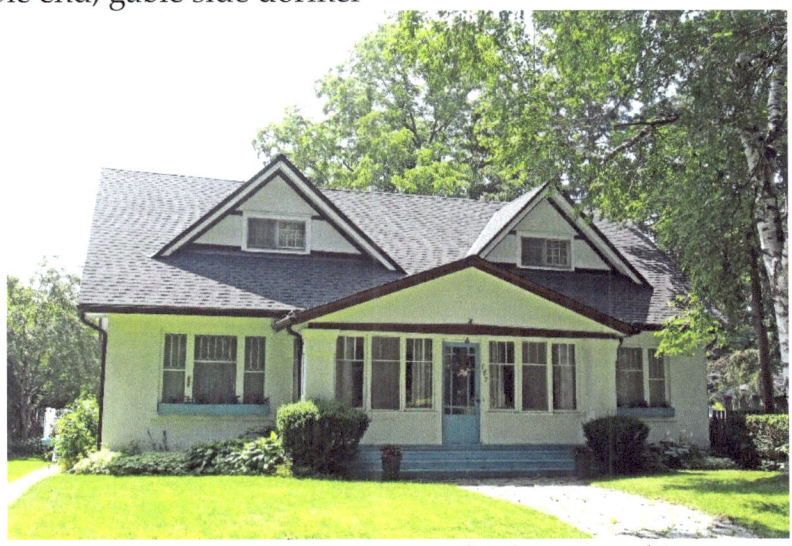

167 Vansittart Avenue - symmetrical 1½ story, white stucco, gable roof, twin gable dormers, paired nine-light square casement windows, windows grouped with leaded beveled glass in top sash, central door protected by large closed porch

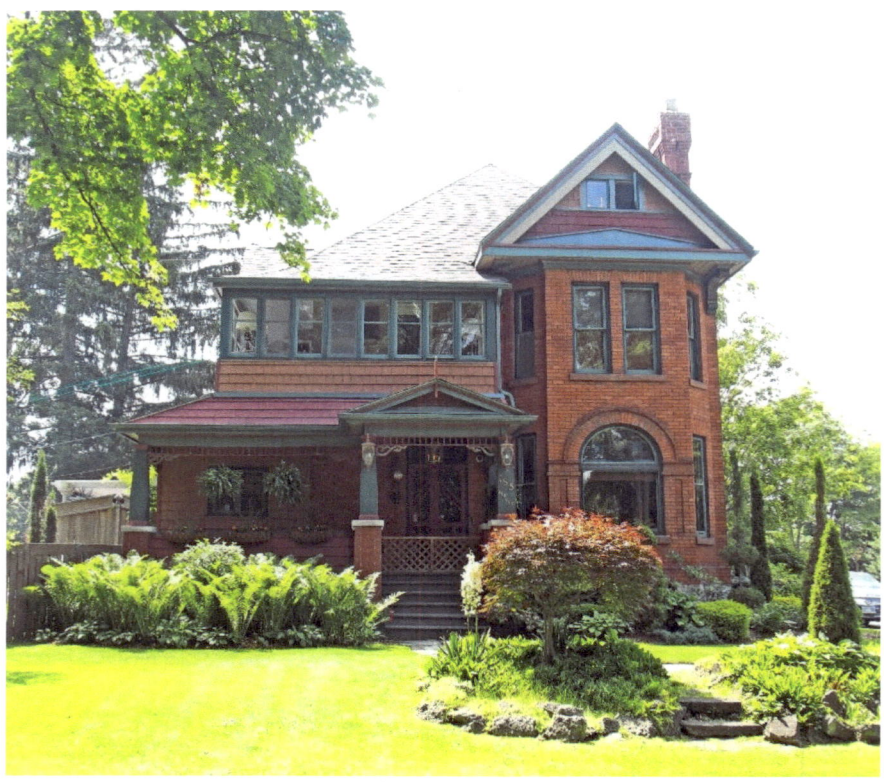

185 Vansittart Avenue – Edwardian - two story with finished attic apartment, red brick, hip roof with gable roof above flat two-story bay window, one-story side bay window, gable ends are stucco and timber, semi-circular windows in first floor bay windows, second floor door leads to open balcony above side bay windows, closed balcony above front open verandah supported on tapered posts on brick pedestals, bell shape painted shingles for balusters, cut limestone foundation

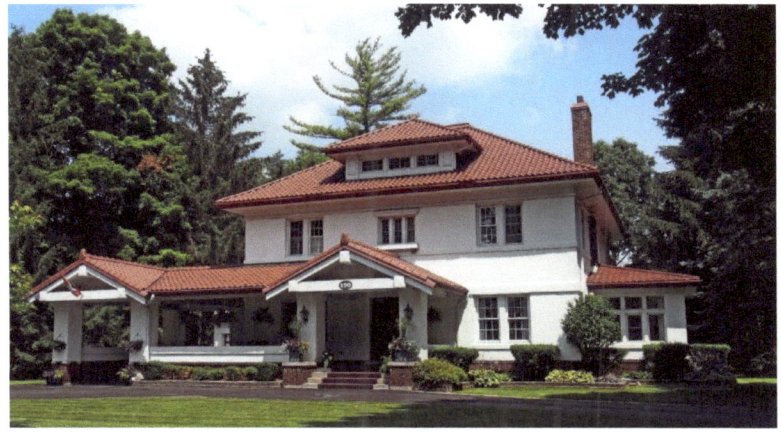

190 Vansittart Avenue – 1926 - Spanish Revival – two story, with attic, white stucco, red tile hip roof with dormer, gable roof on open verandah with porte-cochere for cars

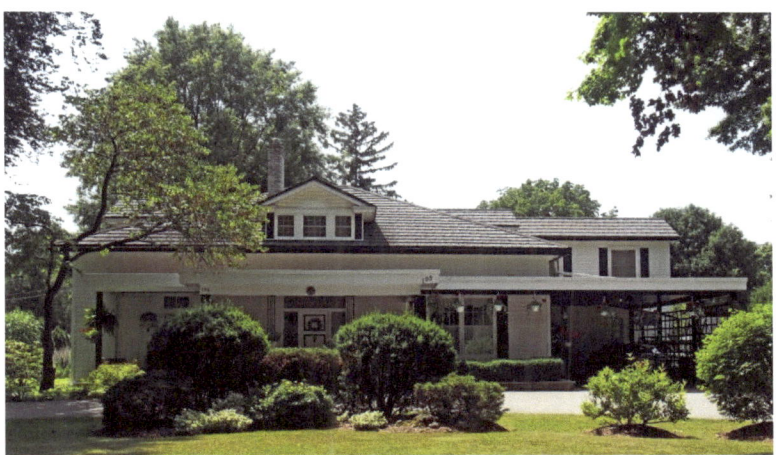

195 Vansittart Avenue 1½ story, dormers and wings added through the years; in 1919 there was no basement when new hot water heating system was added - the men had to crawl beneath the floor boards

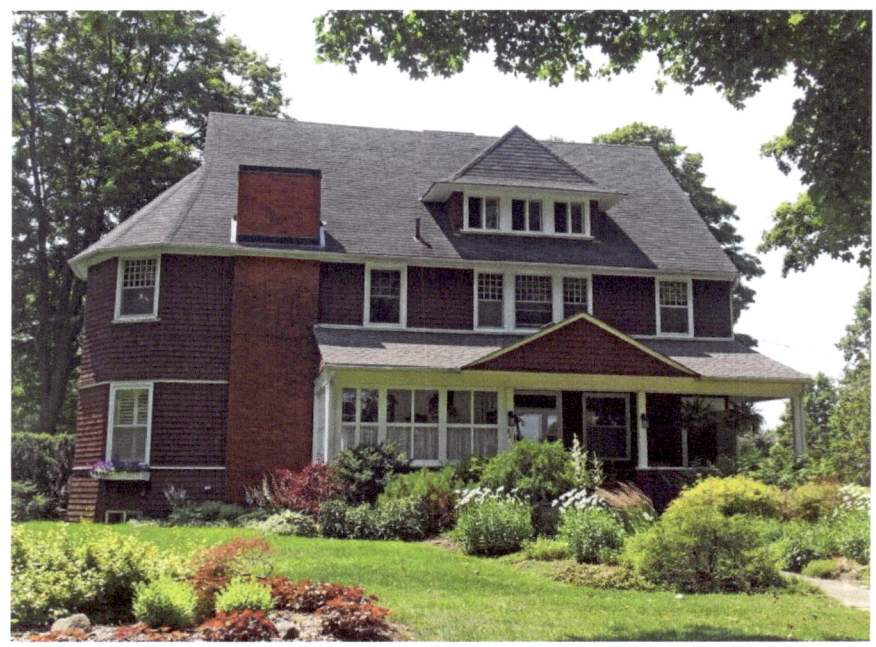

209 Vansittart Avenue – Vernacular - two story with apartments in attic, steep gable roof, south window has diamond lights with lead muntins, pediment verandah is half open and half closed with shingle sides and wood piers

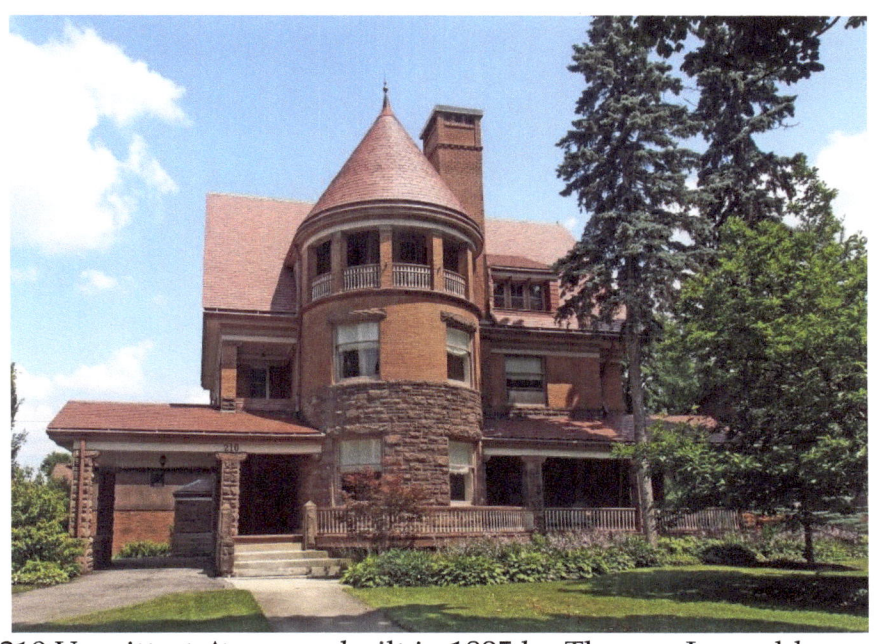

210 Vansittart Avenue - built in 1895 by Thomas Leopold "Carbide" Wilson, inventor of the first commercial calcium-carbide process for the manufacturer of acetylene gas. It was the residence of the Sisters of St. Joseph's until 1975. It is a voluptuous two-story house with finished attic of irregular shape in Richardsonian Romanesque style using contrasting brick, cut stone and hanging tiles - stone main floor, red brick second floor; steep red slate roof, red tiles in gable end and small casement windows, several balconies, large shed roof verandah, brick posts, turned balusters, lattice skirt, a porte-cochere for people to be protected from weather when leaving buggy or cars, off-set tower

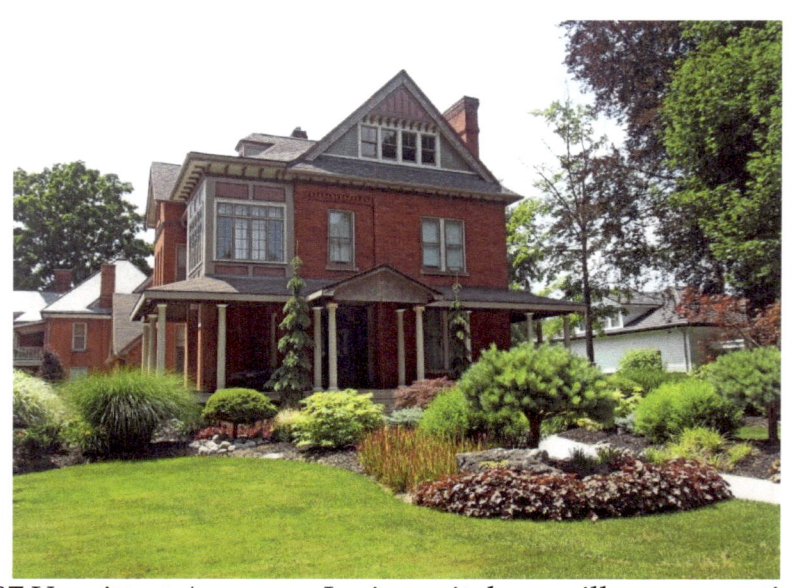

187 Vansittart Avenue – Ionic capitals on pillars supporting pediment, the rest are Doric pillars, saw tooth brickwork, brackets

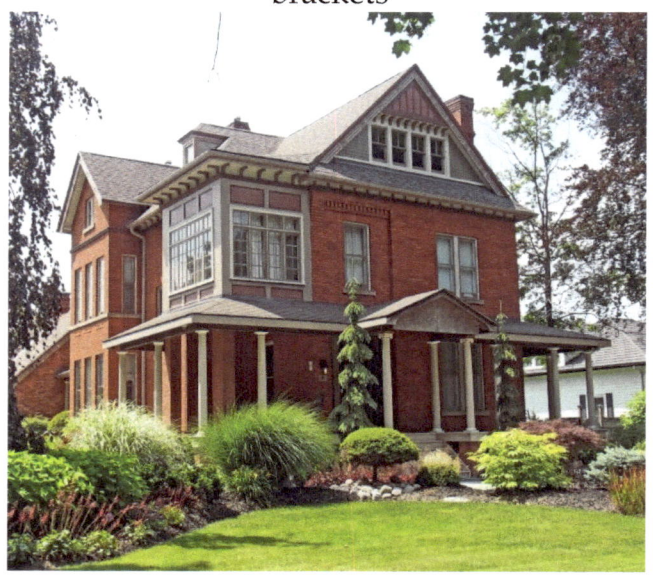

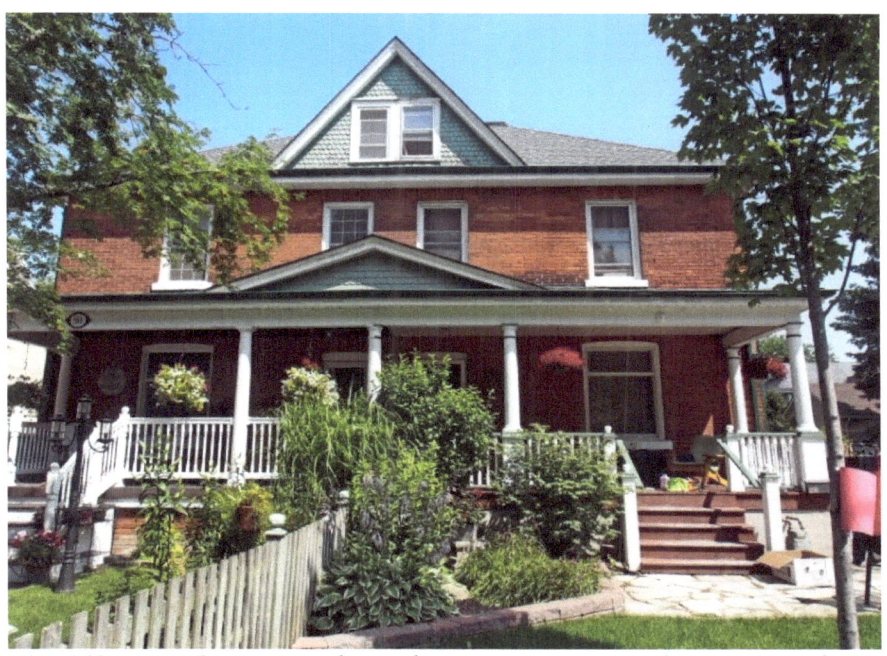

561-563 King Street – Edwardian – symmetrical square red brick two storey, trunked hip roof with front dormer; Doric columns on wooden pedestals for verandah

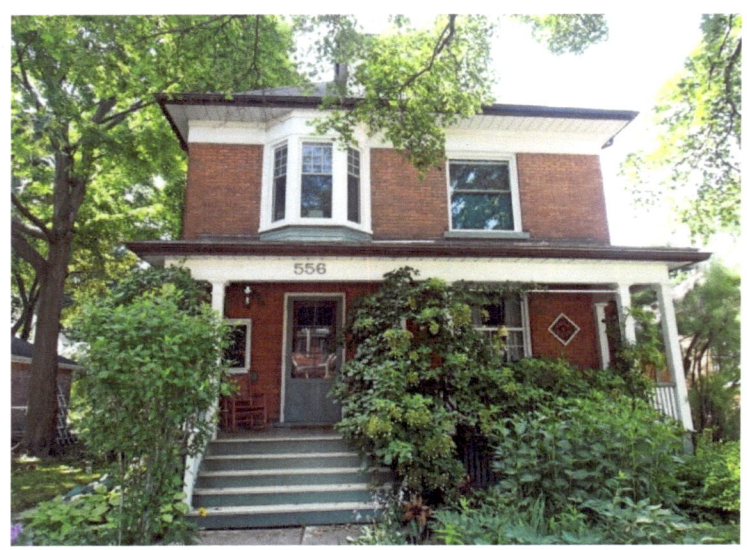

556 King Street – Edwardian - square two story, steep hip roof with front hip dormer, oriel window has upper sash with many lights, Doric piers support verandah, small stained-glass window beside front door

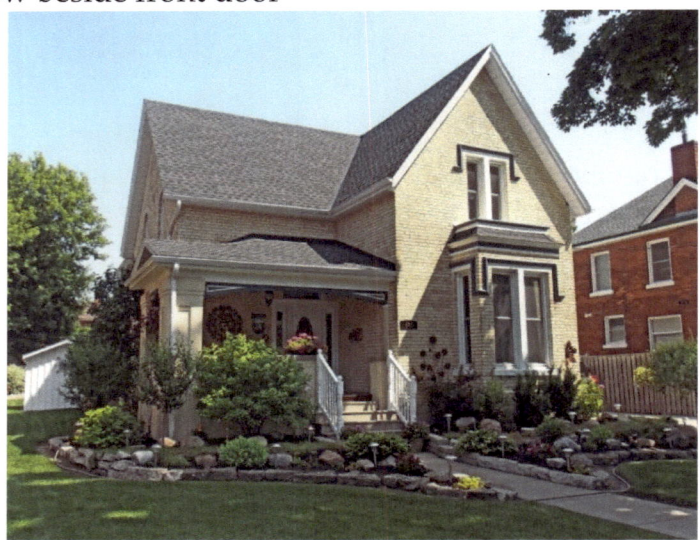

555 King Street – Ontario Vernacular - L shape 1½ story, white brick, steep gable roof, drip molding, first story bay window with flat bell roof, brick piers and walls on porch

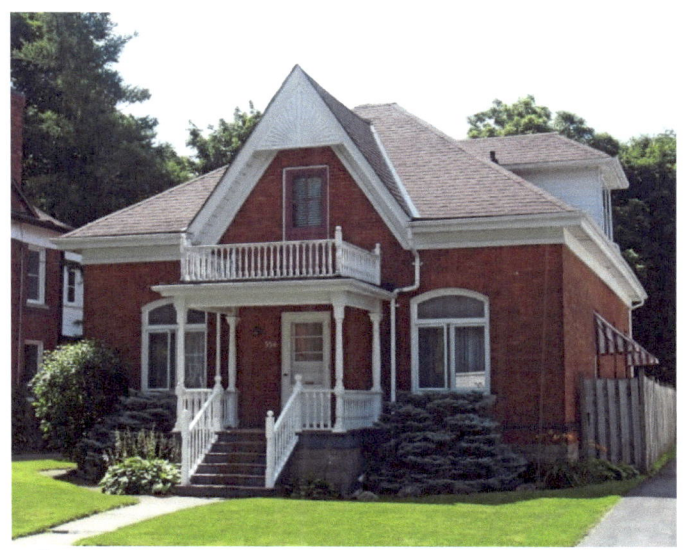

554 King Street – Ontario cottage – symmetrical square 1½ storey red brick house with a steep hip roof; front gable has a decorative wooden sunburst in the peak; open porch with turned posts and balusters with balcony above

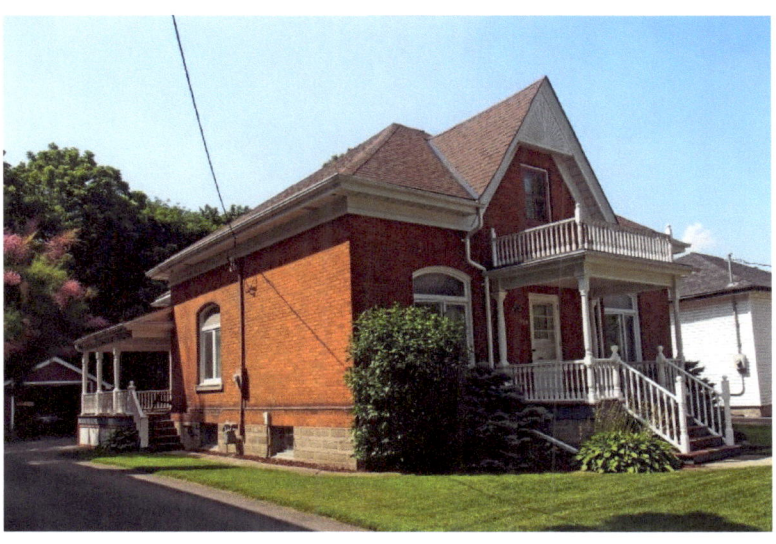

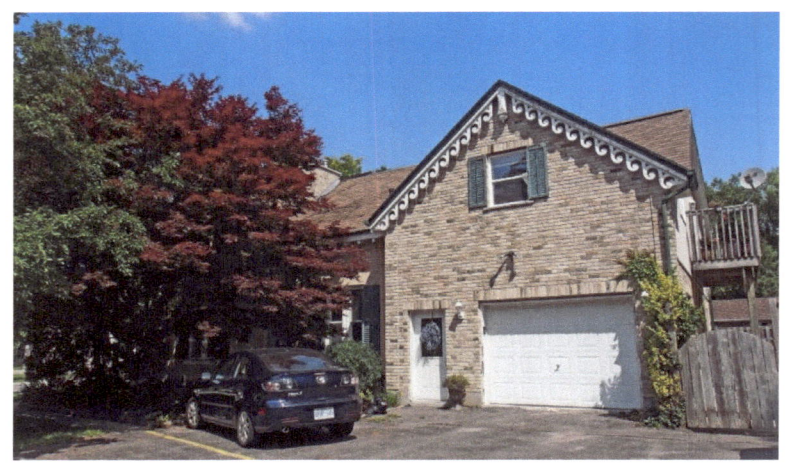

Verge board trim on gable

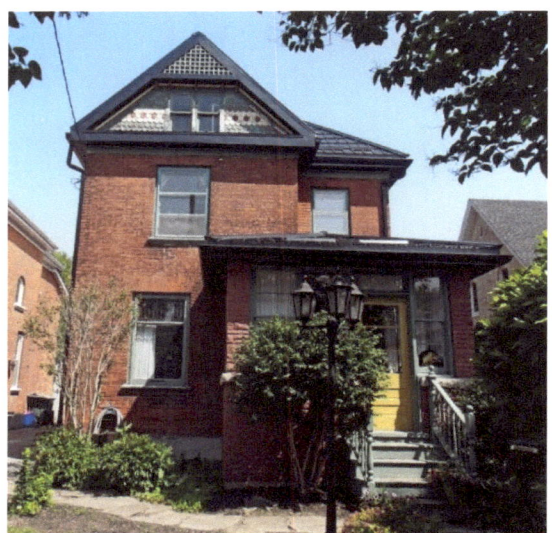

553 King Street – Edwardian - L shape, two story with attic, steep hip roof with gable roof at front, painted shingles and decorative wooden triangle in peak, closed porch

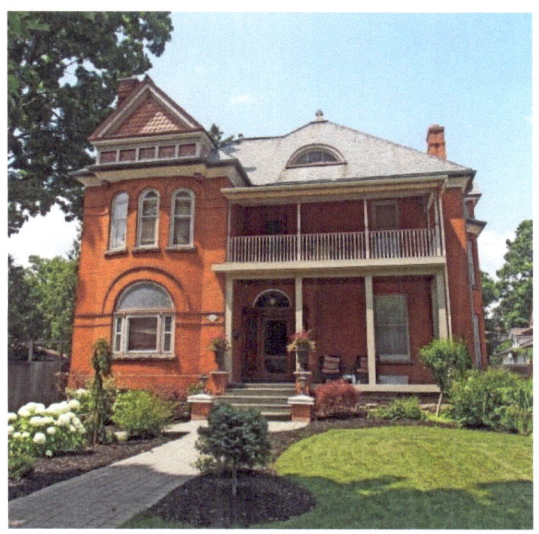

331 Ingersoll Avenue – Edwardian – two story with attic, red brick, finial, front gable has painted shingles, semi-circular and rectangular windows, stain glass semi-circular window and side light for large front window

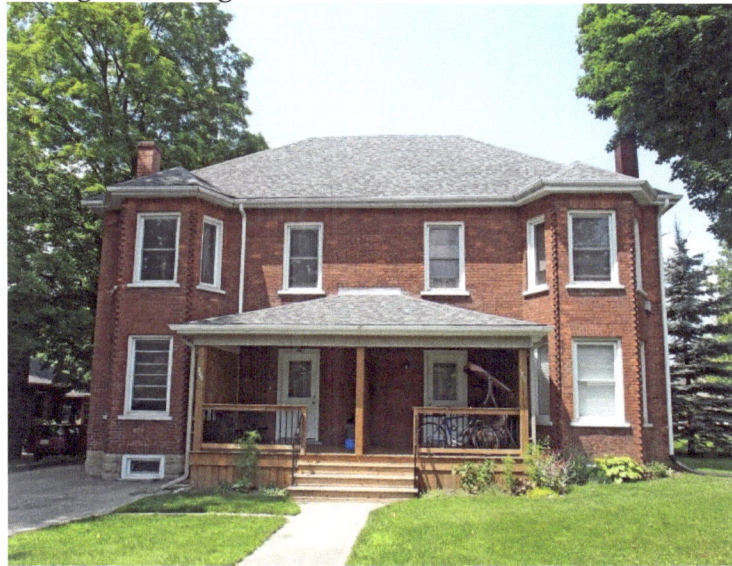

309-311 Ingersoll Avenue – Edwardian - two story, symmetrical, red brick, double house, steep hip roof, two-story bay windows, decorative brick work at corner

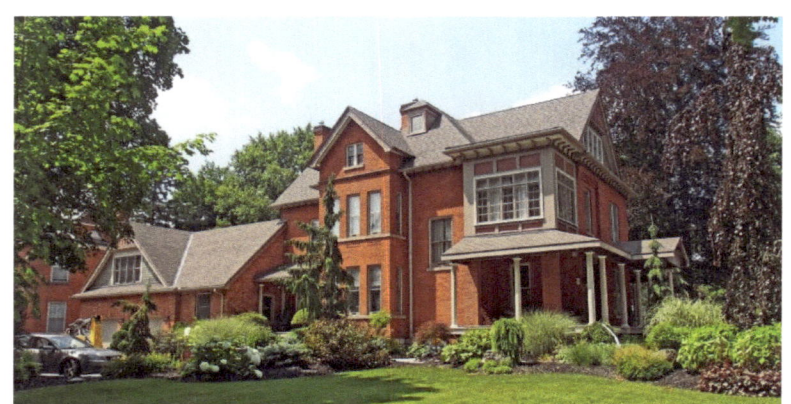

Ingersoll Avenue

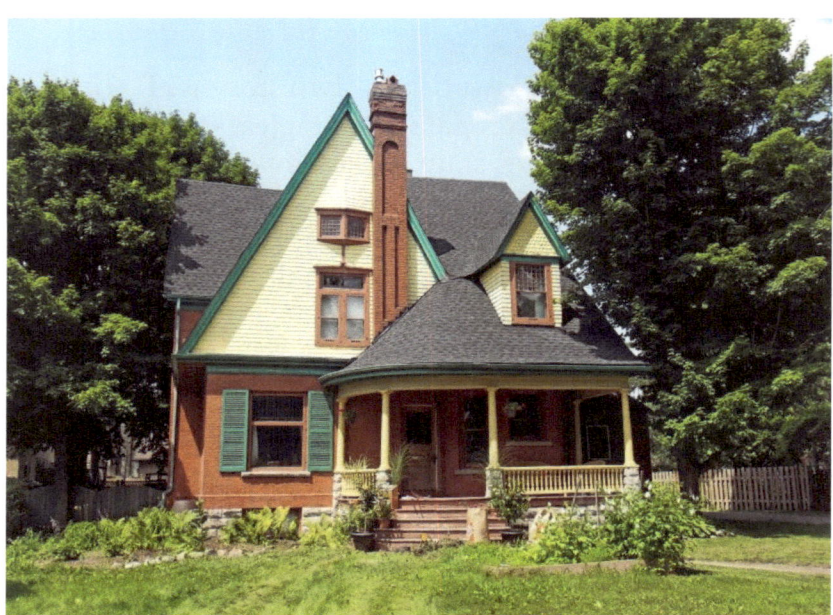

325 Ingersoll Avenue – Queen Anne - two story with attic, red brick, steep gable roof with painted shingles in gable ends, paired window with rectangular transom, corbel bricking in front of chimney, six-sided side tower cone roof, verandah supported on tapered Doric columns on cut stone pedestals, turned balusters

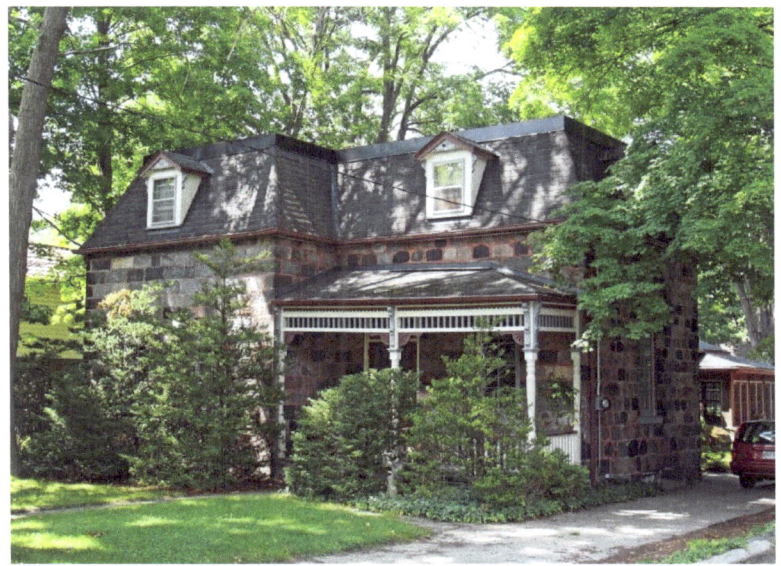

301 Ingersoll Avenue – Second Empire - L shape 1½ story, cut field stone, mansard roof with gable roof dormers, verandah with turned posts, spindles and balusters, double front door

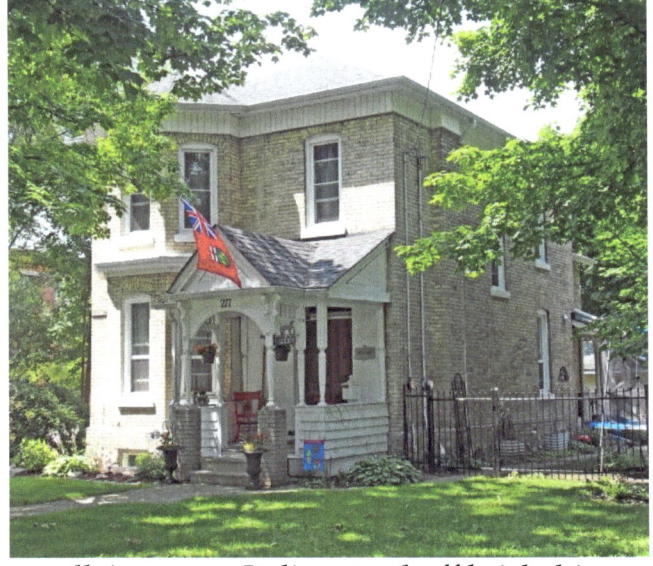

277 Ingersoll Avenue – Italianate - buff brick, hip roof, two-story bay window, turned posts and brackets with spindles

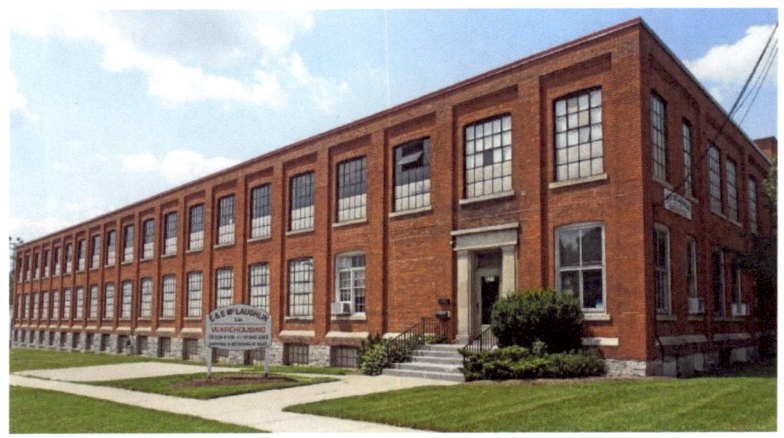

273 Ingersoll Avenue – E & E McLaughlin Warehousing - two story, red brick, commercial building, flat roof, multi-light large, segment windows

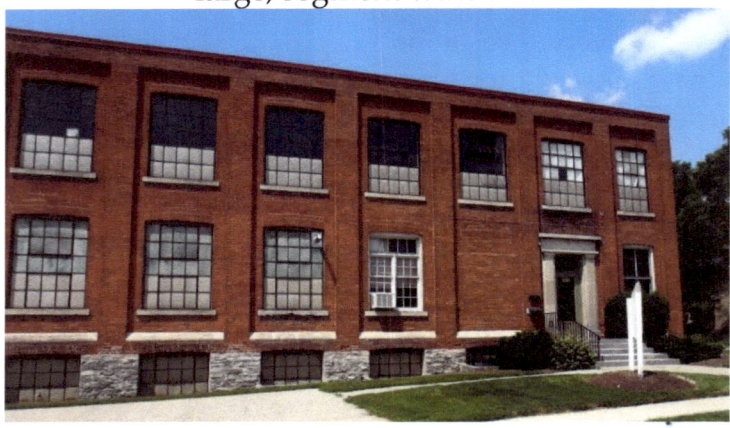

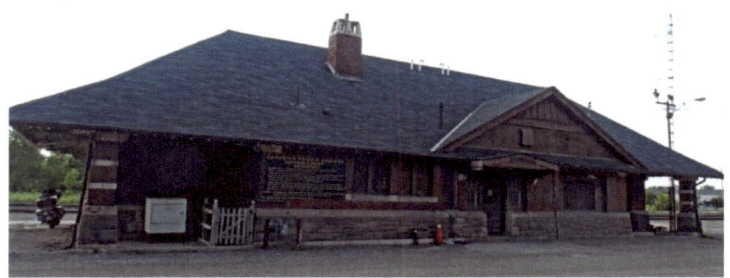

Canadian Pacific Railway Station

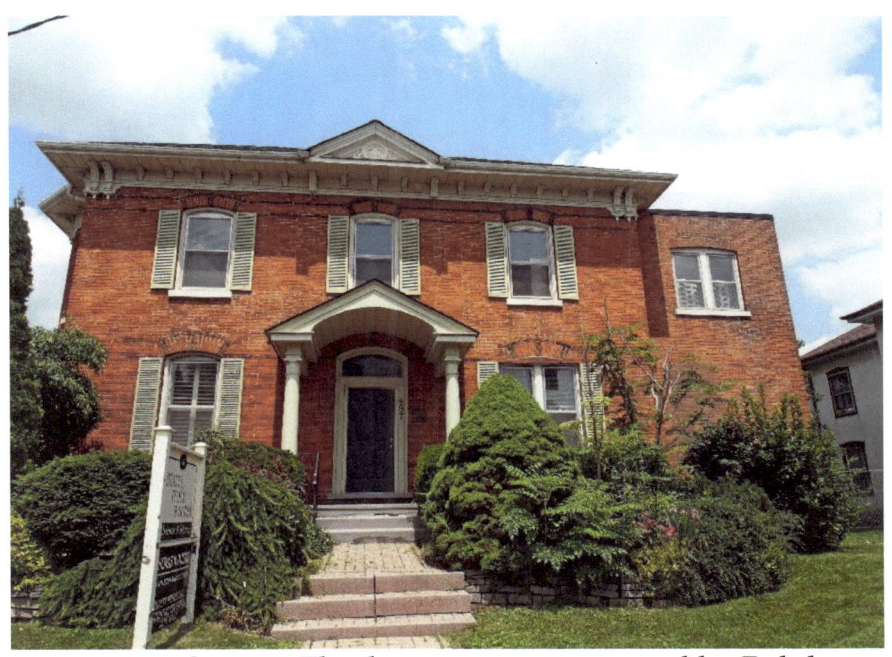

487 Princess Street – This house was constructed by Ralph Bickerton, carpenter and builder, as his family home in 1881. His sons, William John, Robert George, and James Graham, established in 1885 the nationally-known Bickerton Brothers Harness and Saddlery business.

Italianate, Neo-classical - symmetrical full two story, red brick, dichromatic brick accent, trunked hip roof, decorative pediment above entrance, paired brackets on wide cornice with dentils, decorative shutters, centered door with etched glass transom, Doric columns support classical pediment roof

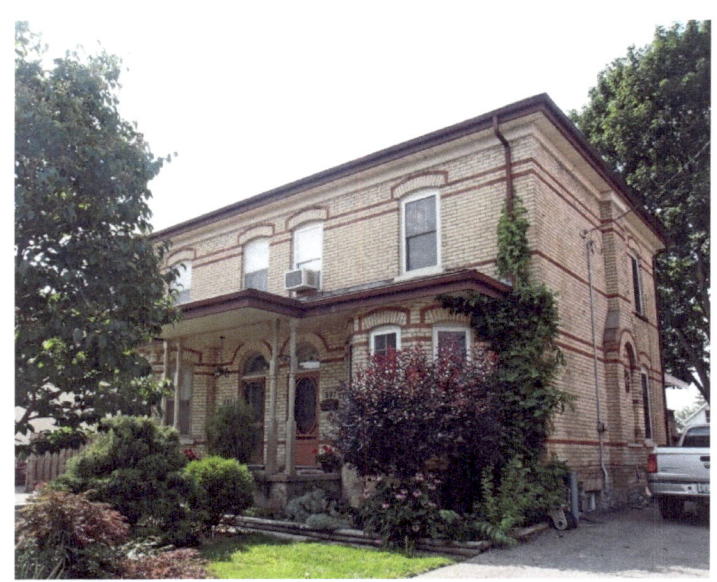

597-595 Princess Street – Italianate - symmetrical yellow brick, bi-chromatic brick, hip roof, one-story bay window, open porch, turned posts, semi-circular transom, centered doors

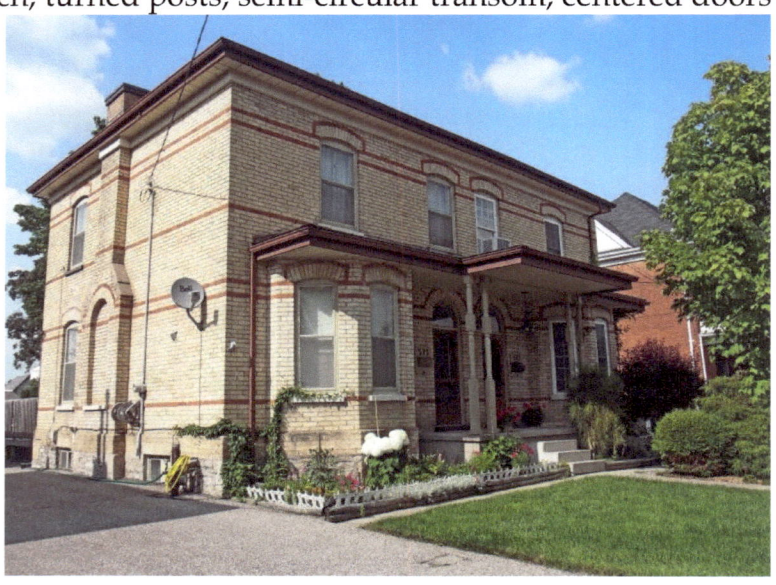

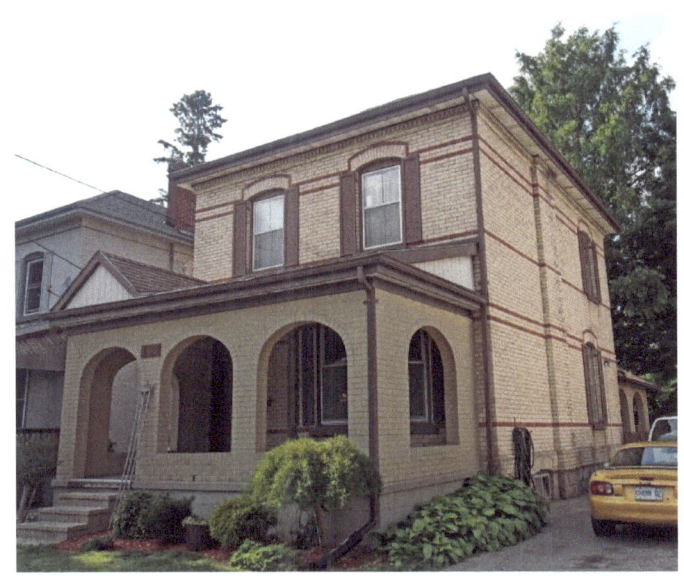

583 Princess Street – Italianate - yellow brick, bi-chromatic brick, hip roof, open verandah with decorative brick arches

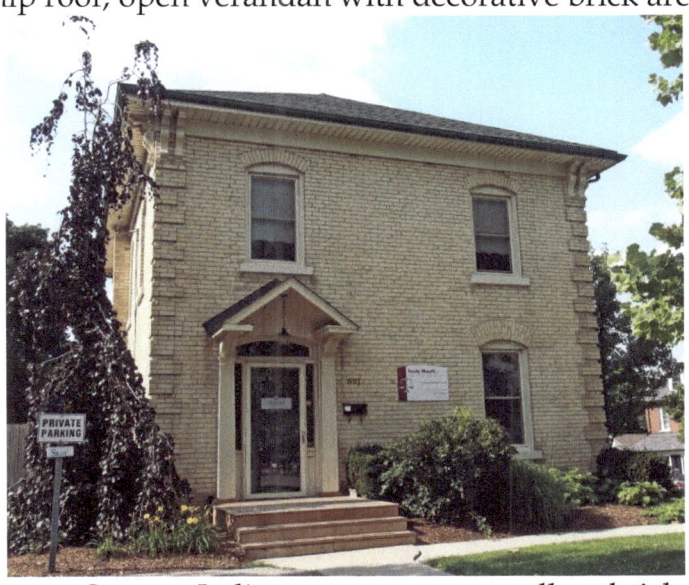

607 Princess Street – Italianate - two story, yellow brick, quoins, hip roof, gable roof hood over doorway with side lights and segmented transom

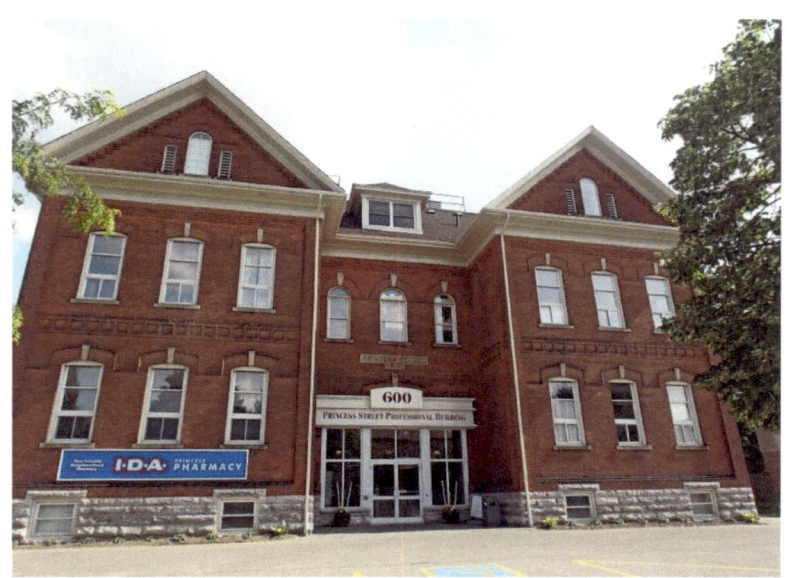

600 Princess Street – Princess Street School -1910 – Neo-classical Revival two story with attic, red brick, brick gable ends with Palladian window, front gable roof, dormer, drip molding above each window, brick lentils with stone keystone, double hung segmented windows, decorative brickwork string course and cornices

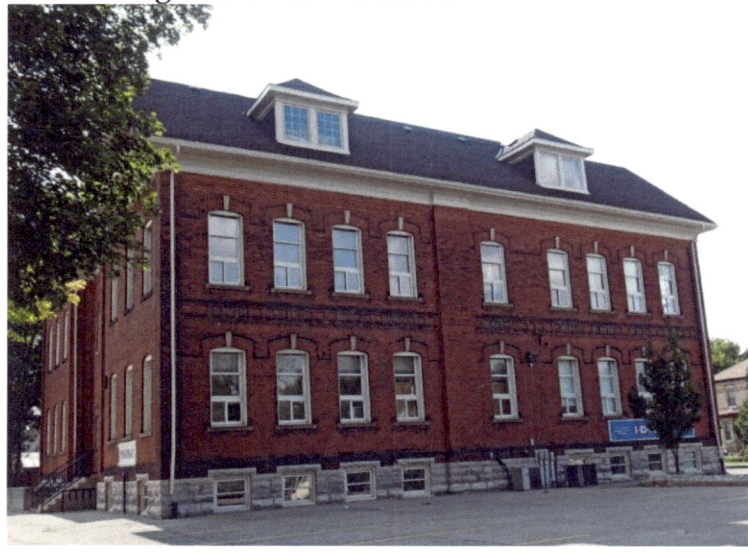

Architectural Terms

Banding: Different materials, colors or textures used in horizontal bands along a wall. Example: 595-597 Princess Street, Page 61	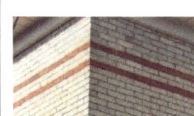
Bay Window: A window that projects out from a wall, in a semicircular, rectangular, or polygonal design. Used frequently in Gothic and Victorian designs. Example: 555 King Street, Page 52	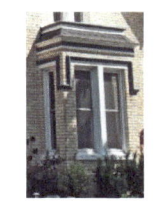
Belvedere: (from the Italian "beautiful view") an architectural feature on a roof, in a garden or on a terrace that gives a beautiful view. Example: 146 Vansittart Avenue, Page 39	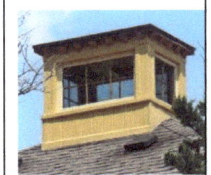
Brackets: a decorative or weight-bearing structural element which forms a right angle with one side against a wall and the other under a projecting surface such as an eave or roof. Example: 410 Hunter Street, Page 9	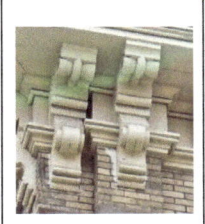
Buttress: a masonry structure built against or projecting from a wall which serves to support or reinforce the wall. In Canadian architecture, they are sometimes used for decoration. Example: 15 Vansittart Avenue, Page 14	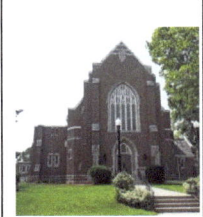

Capital: The uppermost finish or decoration on a column. An Ionic column has a small base, a thin elegant shaft, and a capital composed of volutes which are carved whirls or twists that take the form of a scroll. Example: 187 Vansittart Avenue, Page 46 A Doric column is characterized by a plain column with no base, a shaft with twenty flutings, and a simple capital with a simple entablature. 372 Hunter Street, Page 11	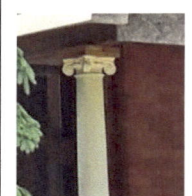 Ionic 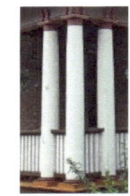 Doric
Cornice Return: decorative element on the end of a gable. Example: 66 Vansittart Avenue, Page 20	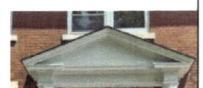
Dormer: (French for "sleep") a gable end window that pierces through the plane of a sloping roof surface to create usable space in the top floor or attic of a building by adding headroom. Example: 81 Vansittart Avenue, Page 23	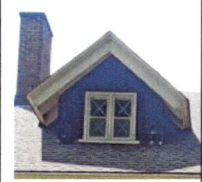
Entrance: The entrance encompasses the doorway and the inner vestibule or, in residential architecture, the covered porch. Example: 415 Hunter Street, Page 5	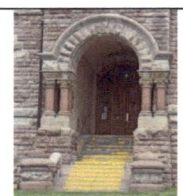

Gable: the triangular portion of a wall between the edges of a sloping roof. Example: 53 Vansittart Avenue, Page 17	
Gargoyle – this is a monkey at the peak of the County Court House. Example: 415 Hunter Street, Page 5	
Hipped Roof: a roof where all sides slope downwards to the walls with no gables. Example: 145 Vansittart Avenue, Page 39	
Iron Cresting: A decorative ornament along the top of a roof. Iron cresting was popular in the Baroque era and also in Italianate, Victorian, Second Empire and Queen Anne styles of architecture. Example: 39 Vansittart Avenue, Page 15	
Keystones and Voussoirs: a voussoir is a wedge-shaped element used in building an arch. A keystone is the central stone that locks all the stones into position, allowing the arch to bear weight. A keystone is often enlarged and embellished. Example: 600 Princess Street, Page 63	
Lancet Window: a tall, narrow window with a pointed arch at its top. Example: 560 Dundas Street, Page 44	

Mansard Roof: This style was popularized by Francois Mansart (1598-1666), an accomplished architect of the French Baroque period and especially fashionable during the Second French Empire (1852-1870). This roof is almost flat on the top section, with two slopes on each of its sides with the lower slope at a steeper angle than the upper and having dormer windows. Example: 393 Hunter Street, Page 10	
Oriel Window - These small areas were originally set into walls and galleries for the purpose of private prayer. Over time, any projecting window or area on an upper floor was called an oriel. Example: 415 Hunter Street, Page 5	
Palladian Window: a large window that is divided into three sections with the centre section larger than the two side sections and usually arched. Example: 47 Vansittart Avenue, Page 16	
Pediment: a triangular section above the horizontal structure (entablature), typically supported by columns. The inside of the triangle is called the tympanum. Example: 34-36 Vansittart Avenue, Page 13	

Sidelight: a window, usually with a vertical emphasis, that flanks a door, and is often used to emphasize the importance of a primary entrance. **Transom Window:** the light above the doorway, also called a fanlight. Example: 66 Vansittart Avenue, Page 20	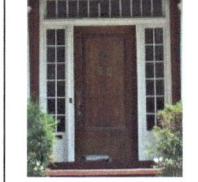
Turret: a small tower that projects from the wall of a building. Example: 95 Vansittart Avenue, Page 26	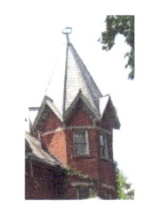
Verge board and Finial: also called bargeboards – hang from the projecting end of a roof and are often elaborately carved and ornamented. **Finial:** ornament added to the top of a gable, pinnacle, canopy or spire – a Gothic element. Example: King Street, Page 54	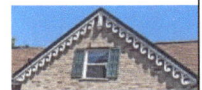
Window Hood: A **hood** is the piece found above window openings, usually of an ornate design, and covers the top third of the opening. Hoods are commonly placed above arched or curved openings on both windows and doors. Example: 393 Hunter Street, Page 10	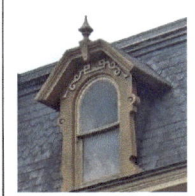

Beaux Arts: Promoters of this style sought to express the classical principles on a grand and imposing scale. Many of the Beaux Arts buildings were banks, post offices, and railway stations. The Ontario Beaux Arts style is eclectic mixing elements of Classical, Renaissance and Baroque. Often the designs have a temple-like façade, porticos with pediments, balustrades, and capitals in many styles. Example: 445 Hunter Street, Page 7	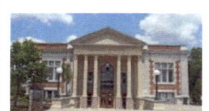
Classical Revival (1820 - 1860) – This style was an analytical, scientific, and dogmatic revival based on intensive studies of Greek and Roman buildings, concerned with the application of Greek plans and proportions to civic buildings. Schools, libraries, government offices, and most other civic buildings were built in this style. Example: 66 Vansittart Avenue, Page 20	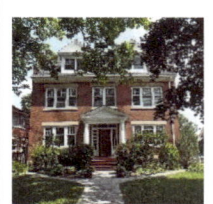
Colonial Revival (1900 - 2003) - an attempt to recall the architecture of the first colonies in North America. Ontario, or Upper Canada, was largely colonized by United Empire Loyalists, English people who were not interested in joining the independence movement of the United States. Colonial Revivals are a tribute to the early settlers. The design is symmetrical, balanced, and refined, often with pedimented porticos, and large Ionic columns. Example: 81 Vansittart Avenue, Page 23	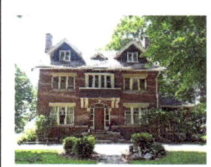

Edwardian, 1900-1930 – This style bridges the ornate and elaborate styles of the Victorian era and the simplified styles of the 20th century. Balanced facades, simple roof lines, dormer windows, large front porches, and smooth brick surfaces are its characteristics. Example: 155 Vansittart Avenue, Page 40	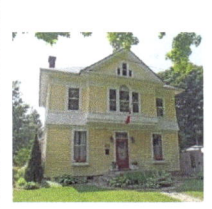
Georgian, before 1860 – This style began with the British King Georges in the 18th century. These buildings have balanced facades around a central door, medium-pitched gable roofs, and small paned windows. Example: 447 Hunter Street, Page 6	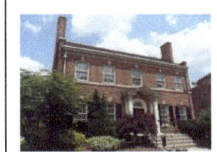
Gothic Revival, 1830-1890 – These decorative buildings have sharply-pitched gables with highly detailed verge boards, pointed-arch window openings, and dichromatic brickwork. It is a common style in Ontario. Example: 15 Vansittart Avenue, Page 14	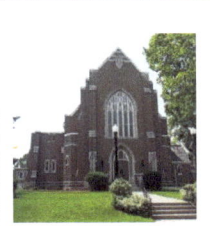
Italianate, 1850-1900 – It has wide-bracketed eaves, belvederes, wrap-around verandahs. Example: 122 Vansittart Avenue, Page 32	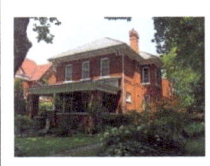

Neo-Classical, 1810-1850 – This style was a direct result of the War of 1812. Many Upper Canadians returning from the war with the United States were second or third generation Loyalists who had inherited land and means from their forefathers. Once the conflict had passed, they had the money and the time to expand their holdings and indulge their architectural whims. Both residential and commercial buildings were constructed on the traditional Georgian plan, but they had a new gaiety and light-heartedness. Detailing became more refined, delicate, and elegant. Example: 410 Hunter Street, Page 9	
Queen Anne, 1885-1900 – This style is distinguished by an irregular outline featuring a combination of an offset tower, broad gables, projecting two-storey bays, verandahs, multi-sloped roofs, and tall, decorative chimneys. A mixture of brick and wood is common. Windows often have one large single-paned bottom sash and small panes in the upper sash. Example: 210 Vansittart Avenue, Page 45	
Regency Cottage, 1830-1860 – This style originated in England in 1815 and spread to Ontario later in the 19th century as British officers retired to Canada. It is a modest one-storey house with a low-pitched hip roof and has a symmetrical front façade. Example: 554 King Street, Page 53	

Romanesque Revival, 1880-1910 – This style hearkens back to medieval architecture of the 11th and 12th centuries with a heavy appearance, blocky towers and rounded arches. Example: 415 Hunter Street, Page 5	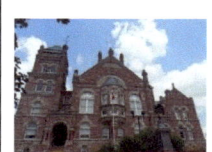
Second Empire, 1860-1880 – The mansard roof is the most noteworthy feature of this style and is evidence of the French origins. Projecting central towers and one or two-storey bays can also be present. Example: 393 Hunter Street, Page 10	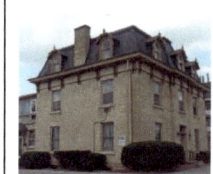
Tudor Revival – exposed timbers with stucco infill, multi-paned windows. Example: 140 Vansittart Avenue, Page 38	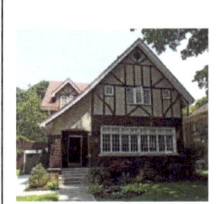
Vernacular/Traditional Mode, 1638 - 1950 Influenced but not defined by a particular style, vernacular buildings are made from easily available materials and exhibit local design characteristics. Example: 209 Vansittart Avenue, Page 44	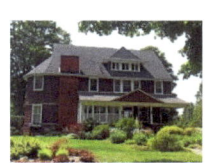

Other Books by Barbara Raue

Coins of Gold
Arrows, Indians and Love
The Life and Times of Barbara
The Cromwell Family Book
Laura Secord Discovered
Daddy Where Are You?

Montana Series
Book 1: Montana Dream
Book 2: Life on the Montana Frontier
Book 3: Montana to Boston and Back
Book 4: Montana Sons Go to War
Book 5: Montana Sons Return from War

Book 1: Rite of Passage
Book 2: Rite of Marriage

Visit Barbara's website to view all of her books
http://barbararaue.ca

www.ingramcontent.com/pod-product-compliance
Lightning Source LLC
Chambersburg PA
CBHW040841180526
45159CB00001B/268